D0299947

Easy Learning

KS3 English Revision

Levels 6-7

Kim Richardson

501 300 155

About this book

This book has been written to help you prepare for your Key Stage 3 English test at the end of Year 9. It contains all the content you need to do well in the reading, writing and Shakespeare papers.

The book is divided into three sections corresponding to the three papers. Each topic is contained within a double page. The left-hand page has all the information and the right-hand page has an annotated example, a sample question and/or an answer to show how the information can be applied in the test.

The sample answers have been given approximate National Curriculum levels and/or a comment for guidance, so you can see the level of the answer and compare it to your own.

Special features

- **Spot Check questions** on every double page are a quick way to check that you've taken in the key points. You can find the answers to these on the inside back cover.

- **Top Tips** pick out some key techniques to help you raise your level.

- **Cross-references** show pages where you can find more information about a particular book.

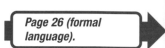
Page 26 (formal language).

- **Did You Know?** items are there just for fun and a bit of light relief.

Revision and practice

Use this book alongside Collins *Easy Learning KS3 English Workbook Levels 3–7*. The workbook contains test-style questions and practice papers so you can check that you have learnt and understood everything from this revision book.

Published by Collins
An imprint of HarperCollins*Publishers*
77 – 85 Fulham Palace Road
Hammersmith
London W6 8JB

Browse the complete Collins catalogue at
www.collins.co.uk

© HarperCollins*Publishers* Limited 2006

10 9 8 7 6 5 4 3 2

ISBN-13 978-0-00-723354-0
ISBN-10 0-00-723354-X

Kim Richardson asserts his moral right to be identified as the author of this work.

All rights reserved. No part of this publication may be reproduced, stored in a retrieval system, or transmitted in any form or by any means, electronic, mechanical, photocopying, recording or otherwise, without the prior written permission of the Publisher or a licence permitting restricted copying in the United Kingdom issued by the Copyright Licensing Agency Ltd., 90 Tottenham Court Road, London W1T 4LP.

British Library Cataloguing in Publication Data
A Catalogue record for this publication is available from the British Library.

Written by Kim Richardson
Edited by Sue Chapple
Design by Sally Boothroyd
Illustrations by Fliss Cary, Linzie Hunter, Andy Tudor, David Whittle, Sue Woollatt
Index compiled by Jane Read
Printed and bound in Malaysia by Imago

Acknowledgements

The Publishers gratefully acknowledge the following for permission to reproduce copyright material:
Extract from *Follow Me Down* by Julie Hearn (OUP, 2003), copyright © Julie Hearn 2003, reprinted by permission of Oxford University Press.
Extract from inside panel entitled 'Protecting ancient forests' in 'Do you share our passion?' Greenpeace leaflet, www.greenpeace.org.uk. Reprinted with permission.
'Death of the Ladette' by Laura Neill, in the *Daily Star*, 10 November 2005. Reprinted with permission.
Extract from RACE AGAINST TIME by Ellen MacArthur (Michael Joseph, 2005) Copyright © Ellen MacArthur, 2005.
Reprinted with permission of A P Watt Ltd on behalf of Offshore Challenges Ltd.
Extract adapted from *Dad Stuff* by Steve Caplin & Simon Rose. Copyright © Steve Caplin & Simon Rose, 2005. First published in the UK by Simon & Schuster UK Ltd. A CBS Corporation.
Extract from p. 41 of *Stone Cold* by Robert Swindells, published by Hamish Hamilton, 1993. Copyright © Robert Swindells, 1993. Reproduced with permission of Penguin Books Ltd.
'Weatherwatch' by Kate Ravilious, in *The Guardian*, 30 November 2005. Copyright Guardian Newspapers Limited 2005. Reprinted with permission.

Photographs

The Author and Publishers are grateful to the following for permission to reproduce photographs:
p. 15 Frans Lanting/Corbis
p. 17 HELLESTAD RUNE/CORBIS SYGMA
p. 19 Reuters/CORBIS
p. 35 Richard Cummins/CORBIS
p. 83, 91 Donald Cooper/photostage.co.uk

Whilst every effort has been made to trace the copyright holders, in cases where this has been unsuccessful, or if any have inadvertently been overlooked, the Publishers will be pleased to make the necessary arrangements at the first opportunity.

Contents

Answers to Spot Check questions are on the inside back cover.

The Key Stage 3 tests

What are the Key Stage 3 tests?

- In Year 9 you will be take national tests in three subjects – English, Maths and Science. Everyone across the country will take the same tests. Their purpose is to measure your progress over the last three years (Key Stage 3).

- There are three papers in the English test: reading, writing and Shakespeare.

The reading paper

- The reading test lasts 1 hour and 15 minutes. The first 15 minutes of this is simply to read a booklet which contains three texts.

- The texts will all be new to you. They are on the same theme (e.g. animals, or communication), but they will be written in very different styles.

- You will be tested on how well you understand the texts, and how well you can comment on their language, structure and purpose.

The writing paper

- The writing test lasts 1 hour and 15 minutes. It consists of two writing tasks.

- In Section A (45 minutes) you do a long piece of writing. You are given 15 minutes to plan this piece of writing.

- In Section B (30 minutes) you do a shorter piece of writing.

- You will be tested on how well you can write, which includes the way you organise your answers. Some marks are given for grammar, punctuation and spelling.

The Shakespeare paper

- The Shakespeare test lasts 45 minutes. You are given one question, which relates to two extracts from the play you have been studying in class.

- You will be given a booklet which contains the question and the extracts from the play that you have been studying.

- You will be tested on your understanding of the extracts, and how well you can comment on them.

Speaking and listening

- Skills in speaking and listening are an important part of the English curriculum. These skills are assessed by your teacher. The assessment is based on work that you have done in class over the year. Speaking and listening are not assessed in the national tests.

What happens then?

- Your test papers are sent away to be marked by outside examiners.

- You will be awarded a National Curriculum level between 3 and 7 for your work across all three papers. The expected level for 14-year-olds is level 5. You should aim for at least a level 6.

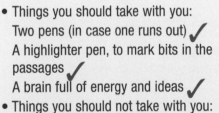

Top Tip!

- Things you should take with you:
  Two pens (in case one runs out) ✓
  A highlighter pen, to mark bits in the passages ✓
  A brain full of energy and ideas ✓
- Things you should not take with you:
  A dictionary ✗
  Your Shakespeare play ✗
  A tired head and an empty stomach ✗

Did You Know?

Although you (and your teacher) probably call them the Year 9 SATs, their proper name is the Key Stage 3 tests.

Spot Check

Discuss in groups the best ways that you have of:
1 planning your revision
2 practising English skills
3 remembering facts (for the Shakespeare paper)
4 handling stress

READING The reading paper

The key things you need to know

- The reading test lasts 1 hour and 15 minutes. It is worth 32 marks.

- You are given a **reading booklet**, which contains three texts.

- You are also given an **answer booklet**, which contains about 12 questions on the texts. You write your answers in the space provided.

The texts

- The three texts will all be new to you. They will be on the same **theme** (e.g. animals, communication or time travel), but they will be written in very different **styles**.

- They will normally be a combination of fiction and non-fiction texts. The non-fiction texts will be in different **forms**, e.g. book extract, newspaper report, interview, leaflet, diary, advert … all sorts.

- The texts will have different **purposes**, e.g. to explain, to tell a story, to persuade an audience, to review a film.

Pages 8, 12, 16, 20, 24 (different types of text).

Reading time

- The first 15 minutes is **reading time**. You use this time to read the texts in the reading booklet.

- Do not read the questions during the reading time. Concentrate on reading the three texts carefully.

- As you read, you can highlight or underline any **key words or phrases**. Also, try to notice **key features** of the texts, such as their structure, how language is used and the mood or tone of the writing.

Pages 10, 14, 18, 22, 26 (key features).

- You don't need to remember everything in the texts. You will be able to re-read the important bits when you answer the questions.

The questions

There are about four questions on each text. The questions will be of **different types**.

- Some questions will be short, and only give you 1 mark each. Others will be longer, and may give you up to 5 marks.

- You may be asked to write a word, a sentence or a paragraph. You may be asked to tick a box, fill in a table or complete a sentence.

- The questions may ask you to:
  - **find information**
  - **comment** on language or structure
  - give your **opinion**
  - **explain** the writer's **viewpoint and purpose**.

> *Pages 28–37 (answering different types of question).* →

Answering the questions

- Start at the beginning and work your way through the questions. The first few questions refer to the first text, and so on.

- **Do exactly what you are asked.** If you are asked to write a word or phrase, don't write an essay.

- Look at the **marks** given for each question, and the **space** provided in the answer booklet. They will give you an idea about how much you should write.

- When commenting or explaining, **refer closely to the text** in your answer.

Top Tip!

You will be tested on:
- whether you answer the **precise** question ✓
- how well you understand the texts ✓
- how well you comment on their language, structure and purpose ✓

You will *not* be tested on:
- your writing style ✗
- your spelling, punctuation or grammar ✗

Timing

- You have 1 hour to answer all the questions. That means about 20 minutes for the questions on each text.

- Use the **marks** as a guide. You shouldn't spend more than 2 minutes per mark.

- Leave 5 minutes at the end to **read through and check** your answers.

Spot Check

Look at these questions. What type of answer is each question asking for? **a** explaining the writer's viewpoint, **b** giving your opinion, **c** commenting on language, **d** finding information
1 Which words show that Sam is frightened?
2 Comment on the writer's use of language to describe how frightened Sam is.
3 Explain how the writer structures the passage to show Sam's fear gradually increasing.
4 What do you think Sam is most frightened of in this passage?

What is fiction?

- Fiction means **stories** which describe imaginary events in a way that entertains the reader. The text on the page opposite is the opening to a novel.

- Some stories have a **message** or **moral**, for example fables or religious stories.

- The key features of a story to comment on are the **plot**, **language**, **setting** and **characters**.

Pages 10–11 (characters).

Plot

- The plot is the **storyline**. Plots often have a similar structure – an introduction, a development (build up), a crisis and a resolution (when things are sorted out).

- **Fast moving** plots are exciting and full of tension. **Slow moving** plots focus more on character, mood and description.

- **Theme** is different from **plot**. Themes are the underlying ideas or issues that the story deals with. For example, the plot of *Private Peaceful* follows the fortunes of two soldiers in World War I. Its **themes** include growing up, bravery, bullying and war.

Language

- Words are chosen carefully to create a precise effect. Writers use **descriptive detail** and **imagery**, as in this extract from the text opposite: *for a moment the page of the London A to Z he was supposed to be reading blurred and swam beneath his eyes.*

- Writers pay attention to the **structure** of their sentences and how they **sound**, e.g. *Quickly he knuckled the wet from his face. Had his mother noticed? If she had, he would say it was sweat. And that he felt sick.*

Setting

- The setting is the **place** and **time** in which the story is set.

- The way the author describes the setting contributes to the **mood** or **atmosphere** of the story. You can see an example in the opening of the extract opposite, which is set in a hot, smelly meat market.

Top Tip!

To get a higher level you need to be able to comment on **how** the setting of a story helps create a particular atmosphere or mood.

Spot Check

1 What are the four key features of stories?
2 Explain what the resolution of a story is.
3 Think about a novel or short story you have read. What is the plot? What are the themes?

Question

This is the opening passage from a novel.

How does the author make the reader want to read on?

It was the stench seeping in through the car windows that bothered Tom the most. Rank and beefy, it reminded him of the way dogs smell after a walk in the rain. Smelly dogs made him think of Goldie, left behind in Dorset, and for a moment the page of the London *A to Z* he was supposed to be reading blurred and swam beneath his eyes.

Quickly he knuckled the wet from his face. Had his mother noticed? If she had, he would say it was sweat. And that he felt sick. It was late morning, the middle of August, and hot enough for even a skinny twelve year old to be melting like a lolly. Add the stink of Smithfield meat market, leaching through traffic fumes, and anyone with nostrils and a stomach in working order was bound to feel bad.

(From *Follow Me Down*, by Julie Hearn)

level
7

Answer

The author tells us just enough so that we can make sense of what is going on, but leaves lots of questions unanswered for the moment. For example, the boy seems to be in a car going through London, and there's a horrible smell from the meat market. But we don't know why he is there, and why the thought of his dog makes his eyes fill with tears.

The language is vivid and powerful, for example the words 'stench' and 'rank and beefy' to describe the smell. The good description draws us in to the story.

Also, we are told straight away what the main character thinks and feels, so we identify with him. The story is 'alive' from the start.

Did You Know?

The author John Creasey wrote 565 books in 40 years. Twenty-six of them were written in a single year!

Characters

- **Believable** and **interesting** characters are central to the success of a story.

- Things happen to characters, but characters also **develop** (change) through a story.

- Characters affect each other. These **relationships** are often the key aspects of a story.

- **Characterisation** means how an author presents and develops their characters.

Describing characters

You can learn about characters in different ways:

- by **how they look**, e.g. *He had small piercing eyes that were set too closely together.*

- by **how they speak**, e.g. *"Found a shilling, huh?" His voice was gruff. "Want to show me?"*

- by **what they do**, e.g. *He sidled up to me, then grabbed at my hand and sank his teeth into it.*

- by **what others say and do**, e.g. *Harriet let out a shriek of laughter. "You really are desp'rate, en't ya?" she said.*

Top Tip!

To get a level 6 you'll need to be able to give your **own impression** of a character, not just describe what they are like.

Dialogue

- Characters' speech is called **dialogue**.

- Dialogue can include different **accents** (pronunciatio and **dialect** (e.g. regional versions of speech).

- Each character will have their own way of speaking, which will be **consistent** through the story.

GOODBYE!

SEE YA!

Narrative viewpoint

- The point of view from which the story is told is called the **narrative viewpoint**.

- A **1st person narrative** is written as if one of the characters is telling it, e.g. *I opened the package carefully.*

- A **3rd person narrative** is told by the author, e.g. *Nasreem opened the package carefully.*

- A **3rd person narrative** is often written from the point of view of one of the characters. The extract on page 9 is written from Tom's point of view.

Read the extract on page 9 again.

(a) What impressions do you get of Tom's state of mind?
(b) How does the narrative voice affect how we feel about Tom?

Answer

(a) Tom is a bit agitated. He is bothered most of all by the smell of the meat market (first sentence), but this makes him think about his dog. This makes his eyes fill with tears (the page 'blurred and swam'), so he is sad.

But he doesn't want his mother to see that he is sad – he is prepared to 'say it was sweat'. Although he is very hot and feeling sick from the smell, this is all he wants his mother to know about what is wrong.

(b) This is a third person narrative, but it is written very much from Tom's viewpoint. We are 'under his skin' and feeling and seeing (and smelling) with him. That makes us want to know even more what he is doing in London and why he is sad.

level
7

Comment

This is a level 7 answer because it shows understanding of all of Tom's feelings. The analysis of the narrative viewpoint is accurate and well written. The student gives a personal response to the text and supports the points made by detailed and relevant reference to the text.

Did You Know?

The evil Professor Snape in the Harry Potter books is supposed to be based on the head of science who taught the author, J K Rowling.

Spot Check

Choose a story you have read recently.
1 Who is the main character(s)?
2 How does he or she (or they) develop through the story?
3 What narrative viewpoint has the author chosen?

Purpose and audience

Some texts try to get the reader to do something, e.g. buy a product, agree with the writer's point of view or act in a certain way. For example:

- Adverts try to **persuade** you to buy an iPod or travel to Portugal.

- Newspaper articles or editorials **argue** that footballers get paid too much, or that we should recycle more.

- Health leaflets and magazine articles may **advise** you on how to eat or exercise properly.

Top Tip!

When commenting on an extract, remember to think about:
- its **purpose** – why it has been written
- the **audience** – who it is aimed at.

Structure

- The writing is usually presented as a series of points in a **logical order**.

- **Topic sentences** often introduce each point.

- **Connectives** show the reader how the ideas are connected, e.g. *however, another point is …, in addition, on the other hand*.

- A powerful **opening** grabs the reader's attention, and a good **ending** has a lasting effect.

Rhetorical techniques

Rhetorical techniques are used to help get the message across effectively. They include:

- **Repetition**, e.g. *Let there be justice for all. Let there be peace for all.*

- Using **personal pronouns** – 'you' addresses the audience directly; 'we' includes the audience on the writer's side.

- **Rhetorical questions**, e.g. *Are we going to give up?* or *Isn't it better that …?*

- **Sound effects**, e.g. alliteration (*nuisance neighbours*) and rhyme (*a bad law, not a mad law*).

- **Emotive language** – language designed to make the audience feel something strongly, e.g. *They are destroying children's lives.*

Design and layout

Adverts and leaflets have **visual appeal**. This makes them attractive and easy to read. Here are some features to comment on:

- **Pictures** In an advert, the picture may be more important than the text.

- **Columns** The text is often in columns to make it easy to read.

- **Design** Colour, font style and size, use of bold/italic, use of space, graphics – all play a part in getting the message across.

- **Subheadings** They break up the text into manageable sections and guide the reader.

Examples

> **Worried about getting spots? The best thing is to eat a healthy balanced diet. It's not too difficult – you just need to:**
> - *have at least 5 portions of fruit and veg every day*
> - *eat starchy foods, such as potatoes and rice*
> - *go easy on the dairy products, such as cheese and milk.*

A typical advice text. Note the conversational tone, direct address to reader, and bullet point list.

> Text messaging is destroying conversation. Have you noticed how people spend the whole time with their noses in their keypads? Not only that, it is wrecking children's spelling and grammar. We should push up the price of texting before standards slip any further.

A typical argument text. Note the clear points made, with reasons, and the rhetorical question.

Did You Know?

The first advert on TV was for Gibbs toothpaste, in 1955. The slogan was, "It's tingling fresh. It's fresh as ice. It's Gibbs SR toothpaste."

A typical advert. Note the appealing image, attractive design and clever slogan.

Spot Check

1 What is the purpose of an advert? Give three ways in which adverts achieve their purpose.
2 What does the connective 'however' signal in a piece of writing?
3 Why do texts that persuade, argue or advise often begin with a question?

Fact

- A **fact** is something that **can be proved** to be true:
  Peter Jackson's film 'King Kong' was made in 2005.
  If people don't agree, you can check facts and show them the evidence.

- An opinion is someone's **point of view**:
  'King Kong' was a fabulous film.
  This cannot be proved to be true. It is someone's personal judgement on the film.

Where you find opinions

You need to look out for **opinions** in all sorts of writing, e.g.

- **reviews** – where the reviewer gives their opinion about a film, CD or book

- **adverts** – where the audience is persuaded to agree with an opinion about a product

- **newspaper** and **magazine articles**, which argue for or against an opinion.

Persuasive opinions

Opinions can be very persuasive:

- They can **disguise themselves as facts**, e.g. *Everyone knows that …*

- They can use **powerful words**, especially adjectives, e.g. *a <u>perfect</u> gift for Christmas*

- They can use **emotive language** e.g. *the holiday of your <u>dreams</u>* or *These men are <u>preying on our children</u>.*

Bias

Writers show **bias** when their language presents an **unfair picture** of something.

- They could **pretend** something is a fact, or **exaggerate** facts or **select** facts in an unfair way.

- They could use a lot of emotive language to **manipulate** our feelings.

Read this extract from a Greenpeace advert.

How does the writer use language to persuade the reader to help the campaign?

> 'staggering' is the writer's opinion. It's a strong word.

> 'ancient' is a powerful adjective that makes us want to preserve the forests.

> 'pristine' (untouched) is a powerful adjective that makes us want to keep our hands off them.

Protecting ancient forests

A staggering 80% of the world's ancient forests have already been destroyed or degraded. Each year, millions of hectares of ancient forests are logged, often illegally, driven by international demand for cheap timber and other wood products, including paper. The UK is Europe's worst offender, with up to 50% of our tropical plywood coming from Indonesia's pristine rainforests. In Indonesia, an estimated 80% of the orang-utan's natural habitats have been wiped out in the last 20 years.

> Facts are given in the form of figures, though 'up to 50%' is a bit vague.

> The reference to orang-utan being 'wiped out' is emotive language. The word LOVE in the photo is also emotive.

Top Tip!

- To gain average marks you must **show the techniques** a writer has used to persuade the audience.
- To gain top marks you need to **explain how the writer has used** those techniques.

Did You Know?

It has been estimated that there are over a million words in the English language – over two million if all scientific terms are included.

Spot Check

1 Are these facts or opinions?
   a It makes no difference if you skip breakfast.
   b Some people eat eggs and bacon for breakfast.
2 Explain how these newspaper headlines about GM food are biased.

FRANKENSTEIN FOODS   FOOD TO FEED OUR FUTURE

INFORMATION

Look out for these key features:

Purpose and audience

- **Information** texts include reference books, travel guides and leaflets.

- Their **purpose** is to give information about people, places and things.

- The **audience** is people who want to find out about something.

Structure

- Clear **organisation** and **logical order** of topics. **Subheadings** and other **presentational devices** guide reader.

- **General statements** or **main points** first, then examples.

- **Tables** and **diagrams** might add information.

Language

- **Present tense** and **3rd person** (*he, she, it*) used, unless it is information about the past.

- Clear, concise sentences.

- Usually **formal** English, and can include specialist words.

Top Tip!

If you are asked to comment on the layout of an information leaflet, think about the images, colours, font style and size, as well as how the images and writing work together.

RECOUNT

Look out for these key features:

Purpose and audience

- **Recount** texts include newspaper reports, travel writing and biography.

- Their **purpose** is to retell events.

- Their **audience** is people who want to find out what happened, and often to be entertained.

Structure

- Events are told in **chronological order**.

- **Time connectives** guide the reader, e.g. *then* or *the following day*.

- New **paragraphs** mark a change of focus, such as a new time, place or person.

Language

- **Past tense**, though present tense can be used in newspaper stories.

- **Descriptive language** to bring events to life, e.g. adjectives, powerful verbs, imagery.

 Page 18.

- Specific **details** given – dates, times, names, descriptions, etc.

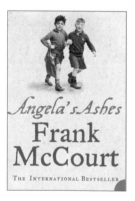

Example

Articles in popular newspapers give information in a particular way:

Catchy **headline** in full caps draws reader in.

Subheading tells you more about the subject of the article.

By-line gives reporter's name.

1st paragraph sums up the story. Note bold font.

Next few paragraphs give **more detail**.

Each **paragraph** is only one sentence. More serious papers have slightly longer paragraphs.

Source of article given – a new survey.

Subheading used to catch eye and break up text. Picks up a word from the text.

Quotations from survey given in inverted commas.

Photos and **layout** more important in popular newspaper stories than in serious newspapers.

DEATH OF THE LADETTE

Old-fashioned girls don't want to party

■ by LAURA NEILL

BRITISH women are rejecting the ladette lifestyle for an old-fashioned family role.

They're turning their backs on the hard partying made famous by the likes of Sarah Cox, 31, and Zoe Ball, 34.

Instead the so-called 'new traditionalists' are married with children.

And they put the family before money and career, though they can combine both.

The new generation of 25 to 45-year-olds has been identified in a new survey.

They admire the values of their mother's era and believe in cooking and knitting, which has become trendy with the stars.

Twist

They snub food fads but know enough about health issues to realise what they should and shouldn't eat, according to the study for drinks firm Ovaltine.

Interviews with 500 women in the 25-45 age group found many wanted life to be 'more like the old days' with a modern twist.

Did You Know?

The book ...*All That Men Know About Women*, which was published in 1996, has 200 pages – but they're all blank!

Spot Check

1 What is the difference between a biography and an autobiography?
2 Would you expect diaries to be written in the 1st or 3rd person?
3 'News stories in popular newspapers aim to entertain as well as inform.' True or false?

Focus on: what makes a good description

Using the senses

- The senses are: looking, hearing, smelling, tasting and feeling. A good writer will make you use your senses:

  I felt my legs buckle beneath me. The ground rose up and hit me between my eyes. The earth didn't taste too good.

- A **visual image** is particularly important, as it lets the reader 'see' what is happening.

Imagery

Look out for these special ways of creating an image, or picture:

- **similes**, which compare something to something else, e.g. *Each harsh word was like the lash of a whip.*

- **metaphors**, which describe something as something else, e.g. *His body was a finely tuned machine which needed constant maintenance.*

- **personification**, which describes non-human things as if they were people, e.g. *The wind provided a helping hand as he cycled up the final hill.*

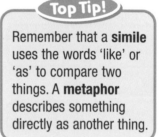

Top Tip!

Remember that a **simile** uses the words 'like' or 'as' to compare two things. A **metaphor** describes something directly as another thing.

Other descriptive devices

- **Powerful words**, especially adjectives and verbs, e.g. *The eagle plummeted into the bleak landscape.*

- **Alliteration**, e.g. *Defeated and disgraced, he stepped out of the ring.*

- **Detail and elaboration,** which adds weight to a description and makes it vivid.

- **Varied sentences** – using sentences of different lengths and types.

Spot Check

1 What kind of imagery are the following:
   a On the morning of my exam the sun rose reluctantly.
   b The flames of her hair crackled as she tossed her head.
   c He used his pen like a sword to attack his critics.
2 Explain how each one is an effective description.

Question

Read this email, which Ellen MacArthur sent on day 21 of her record-breaking voyage round the world.

What makes her description of the storm effective?

New Message

Send　New　Attach　Find　Font　Print

To:

Subject:

Last night was a dark night, hard to see anything out there – nothing but the constant noise of B&Q[1] speeding through the water, the howling wind and the breaking of the waves. The waves are so steep here that poor B&Q feels like she's either running down a hill or being pushed hard up one. Waves regularly break on the windward float quarter. What is noticeable through the dark, shining brighter than our glowing instruments, are the crests of phosphorescence[2] – unbelievable, beautiful, and at times immense. We spend our time, even when trying to rest huddled in a ball in the cuddy[3], just feeling where we are on each mountain, how fast, how far and when will we hit the bottom …

---

[1] Ellen's boat
[2] tiny sea creatures that glow in the dark
[3] small sheltered area on board

Answer

It is a good description because Ellen uses <u>senses</u>. She makes us see things (the dark, then the glowing creatures) and hear things (the howling wind and breaking waves). She also tells us what she feels like in the last sentence.

She describes the waves as hills, and later on as mountains. This is an effective <u>metaphor</u> as it makes us see how steep they are.

There are some <u>powerful words</u>, such as the three adjectives used to describe the sea creatures, and 'huddled' up asleep.

Finally, Ellen gives some <u>detail</u> about the boat – where the waves break exactly – which makes us picture the scene.

level
7

Did You Know?

There are some unusual collective nouns in English, including an 'orchestra' of computers and a 'kindle' of kittens.

INSTRUCTION

Look out for these key features:

Purpose and audience

- **Instruction** texts include recipes, directions and DIY manuals.

- Their **purpose** is to tell you how to do something in a series of sequenced steps.

- The **audience** is someone who wants to know how to do that thing.

Structure

- A series of step-by-step instructions in **chronological order**.

- May begin with a **list** of materials/ingredients needed.

- **Layout** makes the instructions easy to follow. May include diagrams, a numbered list, etc.

Language

- Uses **present tense**, **direct address** (you...) and **commands**, e.g. *Break six eggs into a bowl.*

- Written in **simple**, **clear sentences**, in formal English.

- Paragraphs are **short**.

- Includes **time connectives**, e.g. *first* or *then*.

EXPLANATION

Look out for these key features:

Purpose and audience

- **Explanation** texts include encyclopedias, science textbooks and letters explaining absence from school.

- Their **purpose** is to help someone understand how or why something happens, or how to do something.

- The **audience** is someone who wants find out how something works, or how to do something.

Structure

- A series of **logical steps**.

- Each new point has a **new paragraph**. **Topic sentences** may introduce each paragraph.

- **Diagrams** or **illustrations** may help help the verbal explanation.

Language

- **Present tense**, though past tense is used if explaining historical events.

- **Causal connectives** to guide the reader, e.g. *because* or *as a result*. Also **connectives of time**, e.g. *next*.

- **Formal language**, e.g. *An electric current is generated by special muscle cells in the fish* (note the **passive**). **Specialist** or **technical terms** may be used.

Page 26 (formal language).

Top Tip!

To gain a level 7 you need to be able to say not just why a text has been written (its **purpose**), but also **how successful** the writer is in achieving that purpose.

Note how this text both instructs and explains.

Opening is written in amusing way, to draw the reader in. Explanation texts can be entertaining.

Note **connectives** 'so' (causal) and 'once' (time).

Formal language – note technical terms.

How to teach a child to ride a bike
"Of course I won't let go," fibs even the most doting dad, puffing away madly as he runs behind his child's bike. A moment later he takes his hand away …

There is a better way. Children are instinctively able to 'scoot', so get them used to the bike by scooting first. Once they grow out of riding with stabilisers, remove the bike's pedals, then lower the seat so your child can sit with both feet comfortably on the ground.

Now they can scoot along using both feet. This way they learn how to balance and turn on two wheels without also having to cope with the destabilising circular motion of the pedals.

(Adapted from *Dad Stuff*, by Steve Caplin and Simon Rose)

Clear description of the **purpose** of the writing.

New point, so **new paragraph**. Note topic sentence.

Imperatives (remove, lower) and **direct address** (your child).

Sequence of points in chronological order.

Did You Know?

The first English cookbook, 'Forme of Cury', was written in 1390 by the cooks of Richard II. These weren't curry recipes – 'cury' was the Old English word for 'cooking'!

Spot Check

1 What kind of text are the rules of the card game Racing Demon?
2 What is an imperative?
3 When is it useful to use the passive? Give an example.

Putting texts together

Structure refers to the way in which a text or passage is put together. This depends on its **purpose**:

- An **instruction** text is made up of a clear sequence of steps.

- A discussion (or **discursive**) text may begin with a general introduction, then explore each point of view in turn, then conclude.

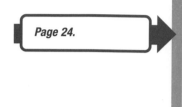

Page 24.

- An **argument** text may begin with the key point of view, then give reasons and evidence, then conclude.

- A **narrative** text may have an introduction, a development, a crisis and a resolution.

What makes a good structure?

- The points are **well organised** – in chronological order (e.g. for instructions) or with the main points first.

- A new **paragraph** is used for each new point or topic.

- Paragraphs may begin with a **topic sentence**, or a general point, and continue with the detail.

- **Connectives** show how the ideas are linked, and where the ideas are going, e.g. *in addition* or *next*.

From start to finish

Structure also refers to the way in which a text begins and ends. This also depends on the purpose of the text.

- The **beginning** may introduce a topic, or draw the reader in with some powerful language or ideas.

- The **end** may sum up the passage (a conclusion), or have a surprising twist, or neatly refer back to the beginning in some way.

Spot Check

1 How do connectives help the structure of a passage?
2 In which of these texts would you find topic sentences?
Recipe, Novel, Information leaflet, History essay
3 How could the end of a passage refer back to the beginning?

Narrative structure

- **Plots** often have this structure – an introduction, a development (build up), a crisis and a resolution (when things are sorted out).

- You may be asked how **effective** the beginning of a story is, or how well the author **builds up the tension** in a passage.

Top Tip!

To gain a level 7 you may need to do more than identify **how** a writer has structured a passage. You may also have to say **how successful** she or he has been.

Question

Re-read 'How to teach a child to ride a bike' on page 21.

How well has the author structured the text to achieve his purpose?

Answer

The passage is an instruction text (with a bit of explanation as well), so the author has made sure that it is organised very logically. He begins by showing you how it isn't done, then he takes you through the steps needed to do it properly.

There is a new paragraph for each point, and the ideas in the sentences are sometimes linked by connectives, such as 'first' and 'then'. This makes the explanation easy to understand.

The opening paragraph is unusual, because it is funny, but it is effective as it makes you laugh and want to read on. The end isn't as successful – there's a very long sentence which is hard to follow.

level 7

Comment

This is a level 7 answer. It covers all the aspects of structure – overall organisation of material, paragraphing and connectives, and the purpose of the opening and ending. It also gives a personal response – the student isn't afraid to criticise the effectiveness of the ending. The short quotations from the text are appropriate.

Did You Know?

In his novel *The French Lieutenant's Woman* (1969), the author John Fowles gives the reader a choice of two endings – a happy one or a sad one.

Reading texts that discuss and review

DISCUSSION TEXTS

Look out for these key features:

Purpose and audience

- **Discussion** (or discursive) texts include in-depth newspaper articles on important issues and student essays in RE or History.

- Their **purpose** is to analyse an issue, exploring different points of view.

- They differ from argument texts because they present a **balanced view**.

Structure

- An **introduction** states the issue to be discussed.

- Each **view**, or point, is explored in turn.

- **Connectives** show the reader how the ideas are connected, e.g. *however, another point is …, on the other hand.*

- A **conclusion** may summarise the arguments or give a personal view.

Language

- **Present tense** and **3rd person** (*he, she, it*), e.g. *Some evidence suggests …*

- **Formal** language and a **restrained tone** – the arguments are presented fairly.

Top Tip!

Most discussion texts are serious – look out for **formal** language. Most reviews are lighter in tone – look out for **informal** language.

REVIEWS

Look out for these key features:

Purpose and audience

- A **review** is a way of **giving an opinion** about a book, play, film, etc.

- It is meant to **inform** the reader, and **persuade** them to buy/read/watch the work (or not!).

- The **audience** of reviews want to find out about the work, and sometimes to be entertained.

Structure

- It often begins with some basic **information** about the work.

- A series of **paragraphs** covers different points, e.g. a book review may cover plot, characters, setting and style.

- A **conclusion** may sum up the reviewer's opinion.

Language

- **Present tense** with **3rd person** when describing the work, e.g. *The film is fabulous.*

- Sentences packed with **detail**, e.g. *It mixes rip-roaring action writing with high-tech funk.*

- Often a **friendly** and **informal tone** to get on the reader's side, e.g. *What a yawn of a book.*

YAWN

Example

Note the features of this discussion text:

Short introduction to the issue.

1st viewpoint. 'Most religious people' signals who hold this view.

2nd viewpoint. 'Supporters of euthanasia' signals who hold this view.

Should euthanasia be legalised?

Euthanasia means deliberately bringing a peaceful death to someone who wants it – they may be terminally ill or in great pain. It is a highly controversial issue.

Most religious people say that only God can give and take away life. These people cannot agree with assisted dying or suicide. Opponents of voluntary euthanasia also say that it is a slippery slope to a situation where the sick or elderly will be killed against their will.

Supporters of euthanasia, however, point out that it is based on the right to choose your own death, which is very different from murder. Furthermore, there are some religious people who support euthanasia, especially in the Netherlands.

For myself, I wouldn't want to live in terrible pain, so I think euthanasia should be legalised.

Title raises the question to be discussed.

Connectives show how ideas are connected.

Conclusion here gives a personal view.

The views are presented **fairly** and in **formal** language.

Did You Know?

Paperback books were not produced until 1935. They were an instant success, bringing books to a much wider audience.

 **Spot Check**

1 Are discussion texts usually biased?
2 When would you use the phrase 'on the other hand' in a discussion text?
3 Why would you read a CD review?
4 If a review covers plot, direction, acting and special effects, what is it reviewing?

Tone

- Tone refers to the **mood** or **style** of a piece of writing, e.g. a light-hearted tone, a serious tone or an angry tone.

- The tone a writer chooses depends on the **purpose** and **audience** of the writing. For example, an advice leaflet aimed at teenagers will have a more conversational tone than a news report in a serious newspaper.

> **Top Tip!**
> To help you identify tone, imagine you are reading the piece of writing aloud. What tone of voice would you use?

Identifying tone

To identify the tone of a piece of writing, you need to look at **word choice**, **content** and **structure**, e.g:

- Colloquial and slang terms give writing a more **conversational** tone, e.g. *in your face* or *street cred*.

- Writing in the 2nd person (*you*) is **more personal** than using the 3rd person (*he/she/it*).

- Exaggeration and jokes and puns add a **humorous** tone.

- Lots of short, direct sentences in an argument text may give it a **hard-hitting** tone.

- Long sentences and paragraphs often add a more **serious** tone.

Formality

Formal language gives writing a **serious** tone. It:

- follows all the rules of English grammar

- uses more difficult or technical words, e.g. *institutions* or *population*

- uses more complex sentences, e.g. *Although he became king in October, it was not until December that …*

- is often impersonal, e.g. *Latest figures show …* or *Steps are being taken to …*

Informal language gives writing a **lighter** tone. It:

- includes slang or colloquialisms, e.g. *cool* or *ain't*

- includes more contractions, e.g. *isn't, can't* or *won't*

- is more personal, e.g. *You could think about …*

- uses simpler words, including 'fillers', e.g. *well* or *yes, but …*

Re-read the passage on page 25.

(a) Give three examples of formal language.
(b) How does the formal tone suit the purpose of the piece?

Answer

(a) The phrase 'voluntary euthanasia' is high level and formalises the subject matter. You would only read this in formal writing.

Some of the sentences are quite complex, such as the one beginning 'Furthermore, there are some religious people ...'. Complex sentences like this are typical of formal language.

Comment

This answer gets full marks. The student has chosen two good examples and shown an understanding of the purpose of the writing.

The connective at the beginning of this sentence ('furthermore') is very high level and formal and leads the reader through the argument.

(b) It is a discussion text on a serious issue – euthanasia – so formal language suits its purpose.

Did YOU Know?

Standard English is the name given to the kind of English you are taught to write in schools. Hardly anyone speaks it, though, except newsreaders on the TV or radio.

Spot Check

1 Describe the two different tones in these pieces of advice:
 – *It is important for everyone's health that they drink eight glasses of water each day.*
 – *Can you up your water intake by drinking up to eight glasses a day?*
2 Arrange in order of formality:
 – *It's really nice.*
 – *It is perfectly delightful.*
 – *That's wicked, man.*

The questions

In the test, some short questions ask you to **find information** in the extract. Often this is the first question asked about an extract.

Here are some examples (about the extract opposite):

1 How long has Ginger been sleeping rough?

2 What part of the country is Link from?

Answering the questions

- You have to **scan** the extract to look for the information you want. Sometimes you are told where to look, e.g. *In the first paragraph, find …*

- Give **only** the information you are asked for, e.g. (question 1):

  - Six or seven months ✓

  - Ginger has been sleeping rough for six or seven months. ✓

  - Ginger has been sleeping rough for six or seven months. He comes from Birmingham. ✗

- Simply copy the key word or phrase that you are asked for. Don't add extra information. You don't need to write in complete sentences.

Top Tip!

- You can rephrase the text to show that you understand it, but it's easier simply to **copy the key word or phrase** that you are asked for.

- Don't spend too long on these questions – they are worth only 1 or 2 marks.

Did You Know?

Rudyard Kipling, the author of *Jungle Book*, once painted his golf balls red so that he could play in the snow.

Spot Check

Look at these statements about questions that ask you to find information. Are they true or false?

1 You don't have to write complete sentences.

2 You need to know information that isn't in the extract.

3 They are worth a lot of marks.

4 You have to put the information in the extract into your own words.

Read this passage about Link, a teenager who finds himself homeless in London. It describes his first night in a street doorway.

I'd just wriggled into my sleeping-bag and dropped my head on my pack when he arrived. I heard these footsteps and thought, keep going. Go past. Please go past, but he didn't. The footsteps stopped and I knew he was looking down at me. I opened my eyes. He was just a shadow framed in the doorway. "This your place?" I croaked. Stupid question. He was going to say yes even if it wasn't, right? What I should have said was piss off. I wondered how big he was.
 "No, you're right, mate." He sounded laid back, amiable. "Just shove up a bit so I can spread my roll." I obliged and he settled himself beside me, so close we were almost touching. It felt good to be with someone. Now, if anybody else turned up it wouldn't matter. There were two of us. I felt I ought to say something so I said, "Been doing this long?" hoping he wouldn't be offended.
  "Six, seven months," he said. "You?"
  "First night."
  He chuckled. "I can tell. Where you from?"
  "Up north."
  "Brum, me."
  "I can tell." It was a risk, this crack about his accent, but he only chuckled again. "Name's Ginger," he said, and waited.

(From *Stone Cold*, by Robert Swindells)

1 What was Link's reaction when he heard footsteps?

2 Link asks Ginger, "This your place?" Why does he think it was a 'stupid question'?

3 What reason does Link give for feeling good about sharing the doorway with someone else?

1 He wanted the person to keep going.

2 Because Ginger was going to say Yes even if it wasn't his place.

3 If anybody else turned up, it wouldn't matter.

The questions

Some questions ask you to **interpret** the text. This means 'reading between the lines'. You need to understand what the author is **suggesting** or **implying** – these things will not be stated clearly in the extract.

Here are some examples of questions like this (all relate to the passage on page 29):

1 Write down two words or phrases which show Link is unsure about the right things to say or do.

2 Give two reasons why Link may have wanted the footsteps to 'keep going'.

3 What impression do you get of Ginger? Refer to the text in your answer.

4 'It was a risk, this crack about his accent.' What does Link mean?

Answering the questions

- Sometimes you are simply asked to scan for the right **words or phrases**, e.g. (question 1):

  'Stupid question', 'I felt I ought to say something'

- Sometimes you need to give a **longer answer**, e.g. (question 2):

  Link may have wanted the footsteps to keep going because he was frightened of being moved on by the police. Or he may have thought he was going to be attacked.

- You may be asked to **refer to the text** in your answer. This means quoting the relevant bit and explaining what it shows, e.g. (question 3):

  Ginger seems to be very laid back. He doesn't pretend that it is his place. Instead he says, 'No, you're right, mate'. He chuckles when he's talking to Link.

Top Tip!

- If the passage is a **story**, try to **imagine** what the characters are thinking or feeling. Getting 'under their skin' will help you answer this sort of question.
- When reading a **non-fiction** passage, think about what a piece of information is really implying. What consequences does it have?

Spot Check

1 What does 'imply' mean?
2 What does 'reading between the lines' mean?
3 'You can give your own opinion when answering this sort of question?' True or false?

Question

We get different impressions of Link's state of mind in this passage (see page 29).

Complete the following table by writing down three more quotations from the extract and explaining what each of them suggests about Link's state of mind.

Quotation	What this suggests about Link's state of mind
"This your place?" I croaked.	He is worried that he has taken someone else's sleeping place.

Answer

Quotation	What this suggests about Link's state of mind
"This your place?" I croaked.	He is worried that he has taken someone else's sleeping place.
I wondered how big he was.	Link was anxious in case he was going to be attacked.
I felt I ought to say something.	He is nervous about leaving a silence between them.
Stupid question.	Link feels annoyed with himself.

Comment

This answer gets full marks because it gives three suitable quotations and describes what all three quotations suggest about Link's state of mind. The answer shows that the student really understands what is going on in the story.

Did You Know?

Bruno Hauptmann kidnapped and murdered a baby, and was sent to the electric chair in 1936. What gave him away was his habit of adding extra 'e's to the end of words. He did this in his ransom note.

The test: commenting on structure

The questions

Some questions ask you to comment on the way a writer **organises** the text. This means thinking about how it is put together. You could be asked about how the whole text is put together, or how certain features (the beginning, the ending, headings, etc.) are effective.

Here are some examples of questions like this (all relate to the passage on page 29):

1 Why does the writer use short sentences in the first paragraph and longer ones in the second paragraph?

2 Give two ways in which the writer draws the reader in at the beginning of this passage.

3 How does the writer create an atmosphere of tension in the first paragraph?

4 Explain why the writer has followed two long paragraphs with several short ones.

Answering the questions

• Sometimes you just have to give a **reason** for something, e.g. (question 1):

> The short sentences show that Link is tense. The longer sentences in the next paragraph show he is more relaxed.

• Sometimes you need to **refer to the text**, e.g. (question 2):

> The writer says 'he arrived' in the first sentence. We are not told who 'he' is, but we want to know, so this draws us in.

• Note that when you give a quotation, you often need to explain why you have used it. *The writer says 'he arrived' in the first sentence* is not enough on its own, because it doesn't explain the **effect** of the words quoted.

Top Tip!

If the question begins, 'How does the author …?' then you are being asked to **explain** the way the author has used words or structure. Back up each point with a quotation from the passage, and make sure you **explain** why the quotation has been used.

Spot Check

1 Why are paragraphs used in a text?
2 What kind of texts use subheadings, and why?
3 Why is the beginning of a text particularly important?

Question

Read the final seven lines of the passage on page 29.

1 Why do the paragraphs suddenly become much shorter at this point? What effect does this have?

2 Explain why the writer has repeated the phrase 'I can tell' at the end of the passage.

> "Six, seven months," he said. "You?"
> "First night."
> He chuckled. "I can tell. Where you from?"
> "Up north."
> "Brum, me."
> "I can tell." It was a risk, this crack about his accent, but he only chuckled again. "Name's Ginger," he said, and waited.

Answer

1 The paragraphs become shorter because the characters are having a conversation. Each speech begins a new line. It suggests they are talking quickly, in short bursts, especially the very short sentences such as 'First night.'

2 Link repeats the same phrase that Ginger has used, as a joke. He is getting back at Ginger by using the same words.

Comment

This answer gets full marks because it explains clearly why the writer has organised the passage in these two ways. In describing the effect of the short paragraphs, the student has quoted from the extract to give an example.

Did You Know?

One short story by Franz Kafka has these famous opening lines:

As Gregor Samsa awoke one morning from uneasy dreams he found himself transformed in his bed into a gigantic insect.

The test: commenting on language

The questions

Some questions ask you to comment on the writer's **use of language** – the **meaning** of certain words, or the **effect** of certain words.
Here are some examples of questions like this (all relate to the passage opposite):

1 In the first sentence, what does 'mischievous little fellow' suggest that the writer feels about frost?

2 What is the effect of describing frost patterns as 'sparkling sculptures' (paragraph 2)?

3 How suitable is the image of a 'spiky white coat' to describe the effect of rime frost (paragraph 3)?

4 In the whole passage, how does the writer's choice of language make you feel that frost is something attractive?

Answering the questions

• Sometimes your answers will be quite short, e.g. (question 1):

It suggests that the writer thinks frost is fun and plays tricks on us.

• In the longer answers you need to **refer to the text**, e.g. (question 3):

The writer makes you feel frost is attractive by using the image of the artist or sculptor. In the first paragraph he 'paints intricate patterns', and in the third paragraph the patterns are described as 'delicate'. Both of the adjectives 'intricate' and 'delicate' make the patterns sound attractive. He is also described as making 'sparkling sculptures'.

Top Tip!

In your longer answers, it is often a good idea to refer to the words of the question in your answer. For example, the answer to question 3 begins

The writer makes you feel frost is attractive …

This keeps you focused on answering the question, and shows the examiner that you are answering the question!

Read this newspaper article. The author explores the legend of Jack Frost and explains how frost affects the landscape.

WEATHERWATCH

Every winter a mischievous little fellow persists in painting intricate patterns on cars, windows, leaves and rocks. Legend has it that Jack Frost was the son of the Norse god of wind, Kari. Originally he was known as Jokul [icicle] Frosti [frost], which became Jack Frost when he emigrated to the UK.

Cold, clear nights with a light wind blowing and temperatures close to freezing are perfect for Jack Frost. Valleys and hollows receive more visits because cold air sinks into low-lying areas. His favourite places to create his sparkling sculptures include rocky, glass or metal surfaces because they radiate heat and cool more quickly than the air surrounding them. Car windscreens are ideal.

Normally Jack Frost paints delicate, feather-like patterns, otherwise known as hoar frost.

He interlocks ice crystals, which grow outwards from a small seed, such as a tiny lump or scratch on the surface. But if the air is moist (often foggy) and the wind a little more breezy then Jack Frost switches to the rime frost technique. Grainy needles grow outwards, lining themselves up with the wind direction and giving structures like electricity pylons a spiky white coat.

Not everyone blames Jack Frost for their white windscreens. In Russia people say that Father Frost has been – a blacksmith who forges great chains of ice to bind water to earth each winter. Meanwhile in Germany Mother Frost is reputed to have been shaking out white feathers from her bed.

Kate Ravilious

(Copyright Guardian Newspapers Limited 2005)

1 Why does the author use the word 'emigrated' at the end of paragraph 1?

2 How suitable is the image of a 'spiky white coat' to describe the effect of rime frost (paragraph 3)?

Did You Know?

The longest word in the English language is 'smiles'. (There is a mile between the first and last letter!)

Answer

1 The author uses the word 'emigrated' because she wants to suggest that Jack Frost was born in another country, and changed his name when he came to the UK.

2 The image of the 'spiky white coat' is very suitable because it shows how everything is covered in white, as if it is wearing a coat. Also the fur on a coat is a bit like the needles of frost.

level 7

The questions

Some questions ask you to comment on the **purpose** or **point of view** of the writer. They may also ask you to explain the **effect** of the text.

Here are some examples of questions like this (all relate to the passage on page 35):

1 Suggest a reason why the author begins her explanation of frost by describing the legend of Jack Frost.

2 Does the author like frost? Explain your answer.

3 The writer talks about Jack Frost throughout the article, not frost. What effect does this have?

4 How does the writer try to make the reader like frost in this passage?

Answering the questions

- Sometimes your answers will be quite short, e.g. (question 1):

  The author wants to grab the reader's interest at the start with a story.

- In the longer answers you need to **refer to the text**, e.g. (question 2):

  The author seems to like frost a lot. She treats it almost as a person, calling it Jack Frost and saying that 'he' has 'favourite places to create' in. She also describes the effect of frost in a positive way, with adjectives such as 'sparkling' and 'delicate'.

Question

In the passage on page 35 the writer sets out to entertain the reader as well as to explain what frost is.

How does she entertain the reader? You should comment on:
- the topics covered
- the language used
- the way frost is referred to as Jack Frost.

In the passage on page 35

Top Tip!

The longer questions, which carry more marks, may give a **bullet point list** of topics to include in your answer. To get top marks you need to cover all the suggestions. They can also give you a structure for your answer – devote a short paragraph to each one.

Answer

Although this article basically aims to give the reader information and a bit of explanation about frost, it isn't written in a dull or lifeless way. To begin with, the author gives us a bit of interesting information about the legend of Jack Frost, which she returns to at the end. She also describes two different types of frost, which is fascinating.

The language is very well chosen to entertain the reader. There are lots of powerful adjectives (e.g. 'intricate', 'sparkling'). The author deliberately describes things in an interesting way, for example she says 'Valleys and hollows receive more visits' instead of 'You get a lot of frost in valleys and hollows'. This brings the passage to life.

The main way in which the author entertains the reader is by referring to frost as Jack Frost. Frost is not just a person, but an artist who deliberately creates pictures and sculptures. He is described as choosing different methods depending on the weather: 'if the air is moist ... then Jack Frost switches to the rime frost technique'. We imagine a person doing all this, not just something in nature.

Above level 7

Comment

This answer is above a level 7. It shows a clear understanding of the purpose of the text, and explains how the writer uses different techniques to achieve her purpose. It covers all the three areas suggested in the bullet points. It gives evidence from the text to back up the views, quoting where relevant and showing the precise effect of the quotations. It is very well organised and expressed throughout.

Did You Know?

There is a word for the study of bird's eggs: oology (pronounced oh-ology).

If you want to move from level 6 to level 7 you need to show these skills.
(All examples relate to the passage on page 35.)

Answer all parts of the question

• Read the question **carefully** and answer it **exactly**.

• If it asks you to comment on a feature through the **whole text**, then make sure you give a spread of evidence across the text.

• If several **bullet point** 'prompts' are given, cover each point in your answer.

Show in detail how the writer achieves an effect

• Don't just describe an effect by quoting the relevant part of the passage. Add a **comment** showing how the effect is achieved. For example, if you are asked to comment on the image 'forges great chains of ice', you could say, *It is a metaphor which suggests the icy grip on the landscape is long-lasting, strong and hard.*

Show how the features of the text suit its purpose

• Be aware not only of language or structural features, but also of how they are chosen deliberately to suit the **aim** of the writing. For example, you could comment, *The author personifies frost in order to make her explanation/information text more entertaining.*

Identify how texts are organised for a particular purpose or viewpoint

• You need to think about the **structure** of the text in terms of how it helps the writer achieve their purpose. Do the paragraphs get shorter to increase the tension? Does each section begin with a rhetorical question to engage the reader's interest? For example, you could say, *The author has used the device of personifying frost consistently through the article to make it coherent (bind it together) and attractive to read.*

Top Tip!

Look carefully at the key word in the question. Questions beginning 'What' are often asking for information. Questions beginning 'How' are often asking you to describe how language is used.

Read the passage on page 35 again.

(a) How has the writer structured the article overall?
(b) How does the structure help the author's purpose?

Answer

(a) The author has used a different paragraph for each topic. The first one talks about the legend of Jack Frost. The second paragraph describes different places and weather conditions suitable for frost, whereas the third paragraph describes two different types of frost. The final paragraph returns to the legend of Jack Frost, but looks at how the story is told in different countries.

Above level 7

(b) The author organises her article very clearly in this way because she is giving information and explaining how something works. Clear organisation is important in this kind of writing. She sandwiches the more scientific material in between information about legends, which is very clever and satisfying: the author wants to entertain us, not just give dry information.

Comment

This answer is above a level 7. The student shows a high level of awareness of both how the text is structured and how this structure contributes to the overall effect of the piece and the aim of the writer. Every aspect of the question is covered, and detail is given. There is no need to quote from the article. The answer is well organised and well expressed.

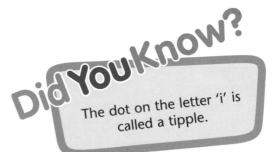

Did You Know?

The dot on the letter 'i' is called a tipple.

WRITING   The writing paper

The key things you need to know

- The writing test lasts 1 hour and 15 minutes. It is worth 50 marks.

- You are given a **question paper**. This contains two writing tasks.

- You are also given an **answer booklet**. This is just lined paper for you to write your answers on.

The writing tasks

- Section A is the longer writing task (30 marks). You have 45 minutes to answer this question.

- Section B is the shorter writing task (20 marks). You have 30 minutes to answer this question.

- Both tasks give you some **background**, and suggest the sort of things you should include in your answer.

- Each writing task will have a different **purpose** and **form**. For example, you may be telling a story, writing a persuasive letter or composing a report.

Pages 52–3 (different forms) and 62–71 (different purposes).

What you get marks for

- **Composition and effect**
  This means the style, form and language that you use – how interesting the writing is, how well it fits the audience, how well the style and tone suits the purpose of the task, how varied and effective the vocabulary is.

- **Sentence structure and punctuation**
  This means how well organised and varied your sentences are, and whether you have used punctuation to make your meaning clear.

- **Text structure and organisation**
  This means how well organised your whole text is, e.g. use of paragraphs and the order of your points.

- **Spelling**
  This is marked only in the shorter writing task.

Top Tip!

Try hard to spell words correctly in the shorter writing task, as 4 out of the 20 marks are given for spelling. It could push you from a level 6 to a level 7.

Pages 42–3, 46–9 and 52–3.

Pages 48–9 and 54–7.

Pages 50–1.

Pages 58–61.

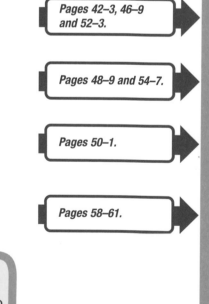

Did YOU Know?

A **blend** is a word made up of the shortened form of two other words, e.g. **heli**port (**heli**copter + air**port**).

Timing and planning

- Your teacher will remind you of the **time**, e.g. when you should be moving on to the shorter task.

- You should spend the first 15 minutes **planning** your longer writing task.

- You should spend the last 5 minutes **checking** what you have written – improving the spelling, punctuation and vocabulary. This will always gain you marks.

Pages 44–5.

Example

Section A
Longer writing task
Building progress

You work for a company that is building a new leisure centre. Your manager has sent you this memo:

Please report on progress so far. Write a detailed report explaining:
- how the different sports and leisure facilities are progressing (quality and speed)
- how well the construction workers are addressing the task
- whether you see any problems with the leisure centre at this stage.

Write a report for your manager explaining what progress is being made in building the leisure centre.

30 marks

As this is the **longer task**, you will be given a grid on which to plan your writing.

The **title** of the task. (This needn't be the title that you give your piece of writing.)

A bit of **scene setting** to give you the background to the task and your role.

This tells you what the **task** is.

Spot Check

True or false?
1 There are two writing papers.
2 You are tested on spelling only in the shorter writing task.
3 Text structure and organisation is about your handwriting.
4 You should spend 15 minutes planning your longer writing task.

Before you plan and write, you need to think carefully about what to write and how to write it. That means asking yourself these questions:

What am I writing?

- Look at the **format** word in the question paper, e.g. Write a **letter**, an **account**, the first chapter of your **story**, a **leaflet**, a **speech**, a **report**, a **newspaper article**.

- Keep this format in mind as you plan and write. Most formats have their own conventions.

- Now identify the **content**, or **topic**, that you have to write about, e.g. (a letter) describing your **visit**, or (a report) describing your project.

Pages 52–3.

Why am I writing?

- Work out your **purpose** in writing.

- **Stories** are easy – they should entertain.

- For non-fiction, though, you must look for the key word in the question: **inform**, **explain**, **describe**, **persuade**, **argue**, **advise**, **analyse**, **review**, **comment**.

Pages 66–71.

Who am I writing for?

- Keep your **audience** in mind when you plan and write. You have to adjust what you are writing to what they want to read.

- The audience is not the examiners, but the **person** (or people) indicated **in the question**, e.g. your fellow classmates, the head teacher, the prime minister, your cousin in America, the manager of a factory.

What is my role?

- You will often be told to imagine you are a **particular person**, e.g. a local resident, a head teacher, a newspaper reporter. This is your **role**.

- Each role will demand its own **voice**. This could be anything from 'very personal and friendly' to 'very distant and informal'.

- The voice you choose also depends on the **purpose** and **audience** of your piece.

- **Get in role** and keep your voice **consistent**. This means:
  - not changing your **point of view**, e.g. from student to teacher, or from 3rd person to 1st person
  - not changing the **formality** of the language unless for deliberate effect
  - not changing the **tone**, e.g. from light-hearted to serious.

Top Tip!

Look at the context when you are told to 'comment'. For example:

- 'Write a letter commenting on the proposals to close the park' means **arguing** for or against the proposals.

- 'Write a report commenting on the results of your survey' means **analysing** the results.

Pages 26–7.

Example

Look again at the writing task from page 41.

How does thinking about purpose, audience and role help you approach the task?

Section A
Longer writing task
Building progress

You work for a company that is building a new leisure centre. Your manager has sent you this memo:

Please report on progress so far. Write a detailed report explaining:
- how the different sports and leisure facilities are progressing (quality and speed)
- how well the construction workers are addressing the task
- whether you see any problems with the leisure centre at this stage.

Write a report for your manager explaining what progress is being made in building the leisure centre.

30 marks

The title of the task gives a flavour of the **voice** you should take on. Here the title is formal, informative and serious.

This is your **role** – you work for a building company. You need to keep this role going through the writing.

This list suggests the **content** of your report. You could **organise** the report into three sections like this.

In the task, you are given:
- the **form** of the writing (a report)
- the **purpose** of the writing (to explain)
- the **audience** of the writing (your manager).

So the report should be clear, formal, logical and polite.

Did You Know?

The most common word used in conversation is 'I'.

Spot Check

1 Match the question with the correct purpose.

Question	Purpose
a Give your views on …	To inform or describe
b Tell x how to …	To persuade
c Give an account of …	To instruct
d Inspire your team …	To argue

2 What does 'keeping your voice consistent' mean?

Planning

Planning is important

- You must spend time planning the answers to both writing tasks.

- Planning makes you **think carefully** about the task, instead of writing the first thing that comes into your head.

- It improves the **content** of your writing. You have time to think up good ideas.

- It also improves the **structure** of your writing. You can organise it instead of just rambling on.

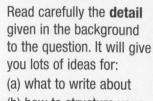

Top Tip!

Read carefully the **detail** given in the background to the question. It will give you lots of ideas for:
(a) what to write about
(b) how to structure your answer.

Planning for the longer task

- You should spend the **first 15 minutes** planning your answer for the longer writing task. A planning grid is provided in the question paper (this isn't marked). Use it!

- The planning grid will often supply the basic **structure** for your writing. You may need to adjust this to make a complete plan (see page 45).

Planning for the shorter task

- You are not given a planning page for the shorter writing task. However, make sure you spend at least 5 minutes **thinking and planning** before you start writing.

- You can use the question paper or some spare paper to draw up a **quick plan**.

- **Brainstorm** some key words and ideas first. Then develop these ideas and order them, using your own planning tool.

Pages 64–71 (planning tools).

Spot Check

True or false?
1 You are given a planning page for both writing tasks.
2 You should spend at least 5 minutes planning for the shorter writing task.
3 Planning helps you organise your writing more effectively.
4 Your planning page is taken in and marked.

Examples

A A planning page for the longer writing task 'Building program' (see page 41).

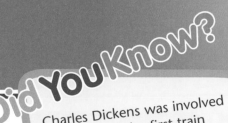

Did You Know?

Charles Dickens was involved in one of the first train crashes in history, when his train plunged over a bridge in 1864. Many people died, and the author never recovered from the experience.

> **How sports and leisure facilities are progressing**
> - swimming pool finished
> - grounds being landscaped
> - tennis courts hardly started
> - main hall under construction

> **How workers are addressing the task**
> - most very hard-working
> - those on outdoor facilities often absent
> - complaints about harsh managers
> - staff holidays will mean further delays

> **Any problems with the leisure centre at this stage**
> - some staffing problems need sorting out: extra cover for holidays, investigate complaints
> - delays to outdoor courts
> - wrong tiles used in main hall

> You can follow this basic structure for your writing, but you will need to add an introduction.

> The notes are short and simple. The order of points in the boxes can be changed when you write your final version.

> This could act as your conclusion.

B A planning page for the question: 'Write the beginning of a short story about someone who has been left on their own.'

> **Notes for description of character**
> - astronaut – unnamed (1st person)
> - normally cool and calm
> - dressed in full gear, heavy helmet, etc.

> **Notes for description of setting**
> - space station
> - set in future, 2500
> - huge area, lots of levels
> - vast banks of computers
> - completely empty – very eerie
> - station circling a new, black planet

> **Notes on what happens in the story**
> - I wake up, after a year's 'frozen' sleep
> - all companions gone – feelings of being alone
> - explore space station, signs that it was left in a hurry
> - computer tells me we're being sucked into dark planet

> This planning page helps you gather ideas for a **story**.

> Jot ideas in the boxes as they occur to you.

> Only this panel can be used to **structure** the story.

The power of words

A wide vocabulary helps your writing in so many ways:

- It means you **avoid repeating** words.

- It makes your writing **more interesting**.

- You can be **more precise** about the meaning or the effect.

- You can use the **appropriate** word for the purpose or audience.

More interesting

- Adjectives and adverbs improve your descriptions, e.g.
  He lay the axe on the ground. ✗
  He lay his battered axe wearily on the ground. ✓

- Longer, more difficult words are often impressive, e.g.
  an atrocious attack, un unacceptable request.

More precise

- Try to avoid nouns and verbs that are very general, e.g.
  She ran to the shops. ✗
  She jogged all the way to the newsagent's on the corner. ✓

- The exact noun or verb you use creates a particular effect:
  The cat lounged in the summer house.
  The cat whimpered in the shed.

Top Tip!

When you are checking through your work, don't be afraid to cross words out and replace them with better ones. You will get marks for using a higher level word, even if it is spelt incorrectly.

More appropriate

Choose words to suit the **purpose** and **audience** of your writing:

- more **formal** words for a discussion piece, e.g. *locate, conclusion*

- some **informal** words for a teenage audience, e.g. *cool, kids*

- **emotive** words in persuasive writing, e.g. *broken-hearted, abandoned*

- **technical** words in information writing, e.g. *species, habitat*

Spot Check

1 Think of four alternatives for the word 'bad'.
2 Rank them in order of 'badness' (the worst at the end).
3 Which of these words would you **not** use in a formal discussion?
wonderful, spectacular, fab, delightful, stimulating

Stylistic devices

- To achieve higher levels, examiners will be looking for some stylistic devices:
  - **alliteration**, e.g. *the ridiculous rodent*
  - **imagery** – **similes** (*as dull as a grey Sunday*) or **metaphors** (*his frustration boiled over into fury*)
  - **extended metaphor** – when an image is developed for a few sentences, e.g. *She attacked her dinner mercilessly. She speared each potato in turn. Then the sausages were put to the sword …*

Example

This is a level 7 student's review.

Read the examiner's comments on the vocabulary used.

Philip Pullman's <u>spellbinding</u> 'His Dark Materials' <u>trilogy</u> ends with 'The Amber Spyglass', which keeps up the superb quality of writing shown in 'Northern Lights' and 'The Subtle Knife', the first two titles in the sequence. Will and Lyra, the two children at the <u>heart of the books</u>, have become separated, and are being hunted down by <u>terrible</u> powers. Can they find each other and their friends? Can they complete their <u>mysterious</u> quest before it is too late? The great rebellion against the dark powers that enslave Lyra's world is nearing its climax.

The <u>plot</u>, then, has all the power and surprise of a great adventure story. The pace of the story never lets up. What is most striking, however, is the depth of the <u>characterisation</u>. Lord Asriel, Mrs Coulter, Iorek Byrnison (the king of the armoured bears) and, above all, Will and Lyra themselves are <u>beautifully</u> drawn characters who <u>fully</u> convince, even though the story is <u>effectively</u> science-fiction. The relationship between Will and Lyra moved me to tears.

Comment

- **Correct terms** used confidently (*trilogy, plot, characterisation*)
- More **interesting** and **precise** than *in the books*
- Good use of qualifiers (**adverbs**) to add precision and force (*beautifully, fully, effectively*)
- **Powerful** and effective **adjectives** (*spellbinding, terrible, mysterious*)

Did You Know?

The English word with the largest number of meanings is 'set'. One English dictionary lists 58 uses of 'set' as a noun and 126 uses as a verb.

Making your sentences interesting

Vary the type of your sentences

- Most sentences are **statements**, e.g. *The CD cost £14.99.*

- You can add **variety** by including other types of sentence:
  - **questions**, e.g. *How much does this CD cost?*
  - **exclamations**, e.g. *Only £14.99!*
  - **commands**, e.g. *Buy this CD for me!*

Vary the length of your sentences

- **Short sentences** often have only one clause, e.g.
  Tammy borrowed £5 from her brother.
  They are useful in instructions and straightforward information
  text. They can also add impact after a series of longer sentences.

- **Compound sentences** combine clauses with 'and' or 'but', e.g.
  Tammy borrowed £5 from her brother and didn't pay him back.
  They can make your sentences longer, but avoid structures like *…
  and … and … and then …*

- **Complex sentences** show the links between the clauses clearly
  by using **connectives** such as 'although' and 'when', e.g. *Tammy
  borrowed £5 from her brother since she had left her purse behind.*

- Include **relative clauses** (to add information), e.g.
  Tammy borrowed £5 from her brother, who never let her forget it.

Top Tip!

Remember that every
sentence must make
sense on its own. This
almost always means
that every sentence has a
verb. Only break this rule
occasionally for deliberate
effect. *Like this!*

Other kinds of variety

- **Begin** your sentences in different ways:
  He went to the arcade. He played on the games. He … ✗
  He went to the arcade. After he'd played on the games, he … ✓

- Expand your nouns with **noun phrases**:
  She was given an alarm clock. ✗
  *She was given an alarm clock designed to leap about instead
  of making a sound.* ✓

- Include **adverbial phrases**, e.g. *in the meantime, for
  better or for worse.*

- Make your verbs **impersonal** (e.g. *It is likely …*),
  conditional, (e.g. *If you heat the water …*) or passive
  (e.g. *The water was heated*).

- You can **embed clauses**, e.g.
  Koala bears, although they look cuddly, are fierce creatures.

Did You Know?

You should never write
'would of' or 'should of'. The
correct form is 'would have'
or 'should have', e.g. *I would
have got full marks marks if I
hadn't written 'would of'.*

Look again at the level 7 student's review from page 47. Read the examiner's comments on the **sentence structure** used.

level
7

Philip Pullman's spellbinding 'His Dark Materials' trilogy ends with 'The Amber Spyglass', <u>which</u> keeps up the superb quality of writing shown in 'Northern Lights' and 'The Subtle Knife', the first two titles in the sequence. Will and Lyra, <u>the two children at the heart of the books</u>, have become separated, and are being hunted down by terrible powers. <u>Can they find each other and their friends? Can they complete their mysterious quest before it is too late?</u> The great rebellion against the dark powers that enslave Lyra's world is nearing its climax.

The plot, <u>then</u>, has all the power and surprise of a great adventure story. <u>The pace of the story never lets up.</u> What is most striking, <u>however</u>, is the depth of the characterisation. Lord Asriel, Mrs Coulter, Iorek Byrnison (the king of the armoured bears) and, above all, Will and Lyra themselves are beautifully drawn characters who fully convince, even though the story is effectively science-fiction. <u>The relationship between Will and Lyra moved me to tears.</u>

Comment

- Effective use of **relative clause** to add information.
- **Connectives** embedded in sentence vary the rhythm, e.g. *then, however.*
- **Embedded phrase** for variety.
- **Questions** add interest and variety.
- Good use of **shorter sentences** to break up the flow and add impact .

Spot Check

1 Combine these sentences to make them more interesting:
   Kevin took the bus to town. He pushed through the crowds. He didn't want to miss the start of the film.
2 Now do it again in a different way!
3 Rewrite this sentence using the passive:
   Midge's mother gave him a hard time.

Paragraphs

- A paragraph is a group of sentences on one topic. Paragraphs are used to **organise** your writing and to help the reader **follow your ideas**.

- You begin a new paragraph when you talk about a **new point**, **character**, **place** or **time**.

- Paragraphs are also used to show **different speakers** in a passage of dialogue.

- You show it's a new paragraph by leaving a line space, or starting the new line slightly in from the margin.

Ordering paragraphs

- This is where **planning** is vital. Each main item in your plan will often become a separate paragraph.

- Number the items on your plan to give you a **sensible order** for your paragraphs.

- The order will depend on the **purpose** of your writing, e.g. **chronological** order (for a recount), **logical** order (for an explanation) or order of **importance** (for an argument).

Pages 44–5.

Beginnings and endings

- The **first paragraph** must be effective. It may be a general introduction, or it may grab the reader by creating a mystery or a shock, or by addressing the reader directly.

- Make your **final paragraph** a definite ending. It will leave a good impression. Techniques include:
  - referring back to the beginning (tying the piece together)
  - a clever twist
  - a sharp one-sentence paragraph
  - a question.

Top Tip!

When checking your work, you can add an insertion mark and write (np) where you want to start a new paragraph. Or you can do the opposite – draw a box round text and link it to the previous paragraph.

Signalling where you are going

- Use **topic sentences** to start each paragraph. These give the main point of the paragraph. Then develop the point by adding reasons, examples, etc.

- Use **connectives** and **signposts** to show where your sentences are going, e.g. *Yet ...* (here's an opposite point), *The following day ...* (to tell you when), *Other people disagree ...* (to tell you who).

This example of an advice text gains a level 7 for its organisation and structure.

level 7

How to deal with rejection

When a relationship breaks up, it can be a very painful experience, especially if it happens suddenly. You can feel a shock, almost as if your friend has died.

> Logical point to put at the beginning.

If the relationship was a really good one, it's normal to feel grief that it's over. So don't think that it's wrong to get some of the grief out of your system by having a good cry.

> Each paragraph covers a separate point.

If the relationship is clearly over, don't waste time trying to patch it up. If you go round pleading with your ex-boyfriend/girlfriend to take you back, you're only prolonging the agony. Doing so is more likely to turn them off than win them back.

> Most paragraphs give the main point first (topic sentence). Then they develop the point, e.g. with a reason or example.

Also, one thing people do when they're rejected is to ask themselves what went wrong. Remember that relationships end for all sorts of reasons, and it's hardly ever one person's fault.

> Connectives and signposts show how the ideas are structured.

Finally, don't worry that you'll never make another relationship. When a relationship ends, it can be difficult to imagine there'll be others. But there will be!

> Effective final paragraph.

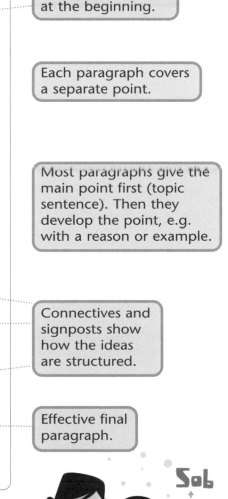

Sob

Did You Know?

The Unfortunates (1969) is a novel supplied in a box. Its author, Bryan Johnson, provides the first and last chapters but presents the rest as single pages that can be read in any order.

Spot Check

1 Give three reasons why you would start a new paragraph.
2 'You need a new paragraph every 10 or 15 lines.' True or false?
3 What makes an effective beginning? Name two techniques.
4 Explain what a topic sentence is.

Letters

- **Lay out** the letter properly.

- Most letters need a **formal** style, e.g. a letter of complaint, a letter to a newspaper, or to apply for a job.

- Some letters will be more **informal**, e.g. to a friend or relative.

Page 53.

Pages 26–7 (formality).

Newspaper stories

- Write in a **clear but lively** style: you need to entertain as well as inform your readers.

- Use **short paragraphs** and **short sentences**.

- The first paragraph often gives the main information – answering the questions 'who', 'what', 'where' and 'when'. Later paragraphs give further details.

- Include **quotes** from people involved, or comments from experts.

- Add a snappy **headline**.

Leaflets

Leaflets usually have to get their point(s) over quickly, clearly and persuasively. Think about:

- **presentation** – bullet points and subheadings are common devices to break up the text. Leave spaces for graphics, pictures or logos.

- **text structure** – short paragraphs and sentences; headings to guide the reader through the text.

- **style** – it should be clear and simple for information or advice. Use emotive words, personal pronouns, etc. for a persuasive leaflet.

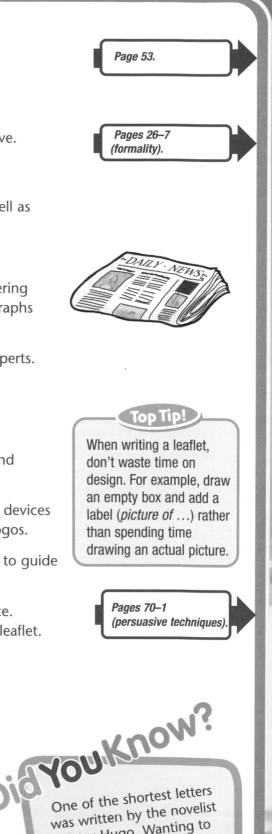

Top Tip!
When writing a leaflet, don't waste time on design. For example, draw an empty box and add a label (*picture of ...*) rather than spending time drawing an actual picture.

Pages 70–1 (persuasive techniques).

Reports

- Most reports are **factual** and **formal**, like a school report or evaluation. They use **clear** and **formal** language, and a **reasonable** tone.

- **Impersonal phrases** are common, e.g. *It is preferable …* or *A good example is …*

- Verbs are often in the **passive**, e.g. *Steps are being taken …* or *The product was assessed …*

- **Modal verbs** are used for evaluation, e.g. *It should take …* or *The manager must learn …*

- The **structure** will be **logical** – introduction, then main points in order of importance, and summary at the end.

Did YOU Know?
One of the shortest letters was written by the novelist Victor Hugo. Wanting to know how people were reacting to his latest novel, he wrote to his publishers: '?' They replied: '!'

Speeches

- Remember that the audience will be **listening** to the speech, so try and imagine someone reading it aloud. Some good **sound effects** include:
  - **repetition**, e.g. *It's time to protest, and to protest with force.*
  - **alliteration**, e.g. *The proposal is dangerous and destructive.*
  - **lists of three**, e.g. *... for a better, fairer and more prosperous future.*
  - **varying the length** of your sentences for effect.

Pages 48–9.

- Speeches are full of **rhetorical techniques**.

Pages 70–1.

Example

Note how this letter is set out.

64 Queensbury Road
Newtown
Yorks YO3 4BX
your address here

15 September 2006
date

Gem Jewellers Ltd
48 High Street
Newtown
Yorks YO1 5FD
address of person you are writing to

Dear Sir or Madam
formal beginning, used if you don't know the name

I wish to complain about the service that I received last Saturday.
clear statement of purpose at the start of the letter

(MAIN TEXT HERE)

I look forward to hearing from you.
You can also use 'Yours sincerely' here.

Yours faithfully

Kara Butler
KARA BUTLER
full name, both signed and printed (in capitals)

Spot Check

Which of these phrases would you include in a letter, and which would you include in a speech?
1 With reference to your advert ...
2 Are we so bad? Are we so mad?
3 Dear Sir
4 I stand before you this evening ...
5 I look forward to hearing from you
6 Listen to reason.

WRITING Punctuation

Basic rules

- Every sentence must make complete sense on its own, so it must contain a verb:
  - *Twenty minutes on the trampoline.* ✗
  - *She was on the trampoline for 20 minutes.* ✔

- Every sentence must begin with a **capital letter**.

- Capitals are also used for **proper names**, e.g. *Raj, Ipswich, Nike, Robston College.*

- Every sentence must **end** with a **full stop**, a **question mark** or an **exclamation mark**.

Punctuation for adding text

- A **dash** adds a short bit of information, e.g.
  I put it here – no, here.
  Do not overuse dashes in this way.

- A **colon** introduces a list, e.g.
  These are our demands: £10,000 in cash, a getaway car …

- A **colon** also **introduces a clause** that leads on from or explains another clause, e.g.
  She was scared: it was dark and very late.

- A **semi-colon** links two clauses that are equally important, e.g.
  Ben liked running; Laura preferred swimming.

- You can **mark off extra information** by using dashes, brackets or commas:
  The culprit – or so it appeared – had slipped away.
  The culprit (or so it appeared) had slipped away.

Pages 56–7.

Apostrophes

- An apostrophe is used where words have been **shortened**, e.g.
  haven't (have not), *I'm* (I am), *he's* (he is), *let's* (let us), *they're* (they are). Note that the apostrophe is put where the missing letter should be.

- Apostrophes also tell you who **owns something**:
  - for **singular**, add apostrophe + **s**, e.g. *Brett's car, United's win*
  - for **plural**, add the apostrophe after the **s**, e.g. *a friends' gathering*

- Do not confuse apostrophes with speech marks.

Top Tip!

Remember that 'its' is used to show ownership (like 'his' and 'hers'), e.g. *She pulled its tail.* 'It's' stands for 'it is', e.g. *It's raining.*

This level 6 writing has some correct punctuation, but needs to improve its range to get a level 7.

level
6

Have you heard people say that soaps are just like real life? However, they are not nearly as realistic as real life, for several reasons. First of all, people die (or disappear) far more often in soaps. This <u>is</u> because of the actors' desire to leave the series after a period. If a key figure wants to leave, the producer has only two options. One is to kill him off, the other is divorce. Secondly, there is always something happening in characters' lives in soaps, whereas in real life it's actually quite boring. The scriptwriters have to make the show exciting to hold the viewers' attention.

> Could add a semi-colon here instead of beginning a new sentence.

> Could rephrase with a colon:
> '… two options: to kill him off or get him divorced.'

Did You Know?

The wrong use of an apostrophe in words that are just plurals is known as the 'greengrocer's apostrophe'. This is because it is so common to see signs like this at greengrocers' stalls.

Apple's half price

Spot Check

1 When do you need to use a capital letter?

2 Add the punctuation to this sentence:
graemes mobile rang it was paula calling from oxford

3 Correct the punctuation in this sentence:
'Its endless is'nt it!' she said – looking at: the minute's go by.

4 What is the difference between a colon and a semi-colon?

What is a comma?

The comma is a very useful and common punctuation mark. It is used in many different ways to **separate words**, **phrases and clauses** in a sentence. Using the comma well in your writing shows:
– that you can **organise** your sentences, so that their meaning is clear.
– that you can use punctuation accurately.

Separating words and phrases

- The comma must be used to **separate items in a list**:
  Please put all clothes, books, swimming and sporting equipment,
  mobile phones and other personal belongings in the lockers provided.
  - Note that the final item before 'and' (*mobile phones*) does not need a comma after it.
  - Note also that the comma comes after phrases (*swimming and sporting equipment*), not just words.

- The comma is used to **separate a phrase** that gives extra information about something:
  The third from the right, the woman in the hat, is the winner!

- The comma is often used **after words** or phrases that **begin sentences** e.g.
  Finally, However, Two days later, After all,

Separating clauses

- The comma is used to **separate clauses** (the main parts of a sentence):
  Although Keith ran as fast as he could, he still came last.
  Rebecca agreed to look after the dog, which was the worst decision she had ever made.

Things to avoid

- Do not put a comma between the subject and verb of a clause, even if the subject is very long:
  The third, final and most important point of all, is that we did our best. ✗
  The third, final and most important point of all is that we did our best ✓

- Think about what really links the clauses of a sentence. Often using a comma is not the best form of punctuation:
  To display web pages you need software called a browser, this converts ✗
  the coded pages into a form that you can read on the computer.
  Here the second clause is just 'tagged on'. You should use a **colon** or a **relative clause** instead of a comma, or start a new sentence:
  To display web pages you need software called a browser. This converts ✓
  the coded pages into a form that you can read on the computer.

Top Tip!
Do not overuse commas. Think about using other punctuation marks as well.

Example

Look at how one student has used commas in this piece of writing.

Lots of girls want to look like the celebrities they see on TV. But celebrities have to look amazing: it's what they are paid to do. Unlike ordinary people, they have the time and money to achieve that perfect look. Most girls would look just as fantastic if they had personal trainers, beauticians, stylists and dieticians at their fingertips. Remember, too, that celebrities use top photographers, who are trained to get the best out of their subject. So don't judge your looks against photographs of top models, as it simply isn't a fair comparison.

A colon here is better than a comma.

Full stops (and new sentences) used correctly here instead of tagging on clauses with commas.

Comma separates items in a list.

Comma used to separate clauses.

Comment

This is a level 7 piece of writing. Commas are used accurately and effectively. They show the structure of the sentences clearly. Other punctuation is used instead of commas where necessary.

Did You Know?

The final chapter of James Joyce's novel *Ulysses* consists of eight enormous sentences. It goes on for over 60 pages and has no punctuation.

Spot Check

Add commas to these sentences:
1 He used the colours red white and blue to which he added yellow as an afterthought.
2 Lucy the youngest of the children is really the most important character.
3 Stuart was replaced at half-time which was the final straw.

Spelling: endings and beginnings

Plurals

Add **-s** to make the plural of a word, e.g. *house → houses, pool → pools*.

Exceptions:

- Words ending in **-ss**, **-sh**, **-ch**, **-x**: you add **-es**, e.g. *glasses, matches, foxes*.

- Words ending in consonant + **y**: you change **-y** to **-ies**, e.g. *lady → ladies, try → tries*.

- Words ending in **-f**: you usually change -f to **-ves**, e.g. *loaf → loaves, leaf → leaves*.

- Some words ending in **-o**: you add **-es**, e.g. *tomatoes, potatoes*.

- Some words don't follow these rules, e.g. *children, women, mice, sheep*.

Verbs

Add **-ing** or **-ed** to make different parts of the verb, e.g. *form → forming, formed; watch → watching, watched*.

Exceptions:

- Short verbs ending in vowel + consonant: you double the consonant, e.g. *drop → dropping; dropped, fit → fitting, fitted*.

- Longer verbs ending in vowel + consonant: double the consonant only if the emphasis is on the final syllable, e.g. *admit → admitting, prefer → preferring* but *benefit → benefiting*.

- Verbs ending in **-e**: you drop the **-e**, e.g. *decide → deciding, decided; state → stating, stated*.

- Many common verbs have different forms in the past tense, e.g. *fight → fought, begin → began, meet → met*.

Prefixes

- **Prefixes** are letters added at the **start** of a word to change its meaning. They do not change the spelling of the original word:

  - **in-**, **un-**, **im-**, **ir-**, **mis-** and **dis-** often form opposites, e.g. *invisible, unfair, impossible, mistrust*.
  - **pre-** and **fore-** mean 'in front' or 'before', e.g. *prefer, foreground*.

- Other prefixes include **ex-** and **re-** (again), e.g. *export, return*.

Your spelling is marked only in the shorter writing task. Don't relax, though – a fifth of the marks in that test go on spelling!

Suffixes

- **Suffixes** are letters added at the **end** of a word to change its meaning:
  - **-able**, **-ible** and **-uble** mean that something is possible, e.g. *legible, soluble.*
  - **-ful** means 'full of', e.g. *careful, peaceful.* (Note: not **-full**.)
  - **-less** means 'without', e.g. *careless, endless.*
  - **-ation**, **-ition**, **-ution** form a noun from a verb, e.g. *create → creation, pollute → pollution.*

- You drop a final **-e** before a suffix that begins with a vowel, e.g. *forgive + -able = forgivable*

Example

Look at these two versions of the same piece of writing. The student checked her spelling at the end of the test and made some corrections.

I don't believe in horroscopes at all. No one knows about the future but Allah. Sometimes the prophesise come true but I think that it's considence. On Wendnesday the horoscope said: "Something aweful will happen today". I worried all day, and then I cought a cold. But surely everyday there's something bad that happens! They're just not believeable.

I don't believe in horoscopes at all. No one knows about the future but Allah. Sometimes the prophecies come true but I think that it's coincidence. On Wednesday the horoscope said: "Something awful will happen today". I worried all day, and then I caught a cold. But surely every day there's something bad that happens! They're just not believable.

Did YOU Know?

'Dreamt' is the only English word ending in 'mt'.

Spot Check

1 Which are the incorrect plurals?
   churches, potatoes, flys, wolves, gasses
2 Add **-ing** and **-ed** to these verbs: *skate, skid, respect, benefit*
3 Give the past tense of these verbs: *dive, steal, travel, buy*
4 Use prefixes and suffixes to form two words from 'believe'.

Use a dictionary

- The best way to master spelling is to look words up in a **dictionary** while you are writing.

- Do *not* use spell checker programs. They don't tell you if a word is spelt correctly, only if it exists. And they make you a lazy speller.

- Note: you are not allowed to use a dictionary in the tests.

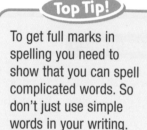

List your spelling bugs

- **Make a list** of words you regularly misspell. Make a bookmark out of it. Learn them.

- **Learn** these commonly misspelt words:
  all right
  believe
  character
  clothes
  coming
  definite
  friend
  immediately
  receive
  separate

Top Tip!

To get full marks in spelling you need to show that you can spell complicated words. So don't just use simple words in your writing.

A freind in need ... *friend*

Beware of homophones

- Some common words **sound the same** but are spelt differently. Learn these and look out for others:

  - *their* (belonging to them), *they're* (= they are), *there* (where)

  - *whose* (belonging to someone), *who's* (= who is)

  - *quiet* (calm), *quite* (a bit)

  - *accept* (take), *except* (apart from)

  - *effect* (noun), *affect* (verb)

Who's clothes are these? *Whose*

Spot Check

1 Which of these words are spelt incorrectly?
quitely, responsible, dissappoint, desperate, beleive, friend, weird, neccessary, occasion.
2 What is the difference between *accept* and *except*?
3 Give a mnemonic that helps you spell.

Other spelling tips

- Master a few **spelling rules**.

- Use **mnemonics**, (memory joggers), e.g. Remember there is **iron** in the env**iron**ment, a **rat** in sepa**rat**e, **finite** in de**finite** and a **cog** in re**cog**nise.

- Group words into **families**, e.g. <u>success</u>, <u>success</u>ful, <u>succe</u>ed; <u>writ</u>ing, <u>writ</u>er, <u>writt</u>en

- **Say the word** in your mind as it is spelt, e.g. Feb**ru**ary, Wed**nes**day

- Break words into smaller chunks, e.g. *ex-treme-ly, re-le-vant*.

Pages 58–9.

Example

A student has checked this paragraph and corrected the spelling in places. Read the paragraph and the examiner's comment.

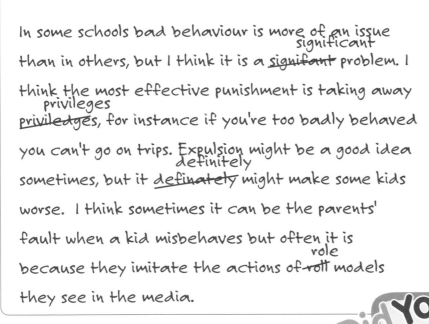

In some schools bad behaviour is more of an issue than in others, but I think it is a ~~signifant~~ significant problem. I think the most effective punishment is taking away ~~priviledges~~ privileges, for instance if you're too badly behaved you can't go on trips. Expulsion might be a good idea sometimes, but it ~~definately~~ definitely might make some kids worse. I think sometimes it can be the parents' fault when a kid misbehaves but often it is because they imitate the actions of ~~roll~~ role models they see in the media.

Comment

All spelling is correct, including complex and irregular words such as *definitely* and *privileges*. A wide range of vocabulary has been chosen. Therefore 4 marks out of 4 are awarded for spelling.

Did You Know?

The first printers added letters to the ends of words to straighten the right-hand edge of their texts. Spelling wasn't so important in the Middle Ages!

Writing a story

Planning and structure

- If you are given a story to write, it will probably be for the longer writing task. Use the **planning grid** on the question paper.

Pages 44–5.

- You also need to plan the **structure** of your story carefully:

  – Give your story an **introduction**, a **development** (build up), a **crisis** and a **resolution** (when things are sorted out).

  – If you want a **fast moving** story, make it exciting and full of tension.

  – If you want a **slow moving** story, focus more on character, feelings and description.

  – Sometimes you are asked to write only the **beginning** of a story.

  – Be daring: *begin* in the middle of the action, then backtrack. Or **end** with a cliffhanger, or a clever twist.

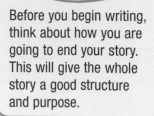

Top Tip!

Before you begin writing, think about how you are going to end your story. This will give the whole story a good structure and purpose.

Characters

- Your characters need to be **believable** and **interesting**. Don't include more than two or three, or they will become just names.

- Describe characters by how they **look**, what they **say** and what they **do**. Often their feelings are better **implied** than stated directly:
  The children felt very cold. ✗
  The children huddled together, their teeth chattering. ✔

- Get **under the skin** of the main character and write from their point of view.

- Keep your **viewpoint consistent**. If you begin writing as the main character (using 'I'), stick to it.

Shiver

Dialogue

- Speech adds **variety** to your story. It also **develops the characters and the plot** and brings both to life.

- Make speech **realistic**. People speak in short sentences and don't always obey the rules of Standard English. Think what *you* would say, and how *you* would say it.

- Follow the rules for **punctuating** speech, and other guidelines.

Page 63.

- Make your sentences **interesting**. Think carefully about the words that you use. In particular:

- Use **adjectives** and **adverbs** to give descriptive detail, especially to create the setting.

- Use powerful **nouns** and **verbs** for effect.

- Include some **imagery**.

- **Vary** the length and type of your sentences.

Page 18 (imagery) and pages 48–9 (variety).

Example

Follow these guidelines when writing dialogue.

Begin a new paragraph each time the speaker changes.

Note how Keith's speech is informal, but Jim's is formal.

Mix speech and action to move the story on.

> The policeman grabbed Keith by the collar. "Not so fast, lad," he whispered in his ear.
>
> "Ow, leggo!" yelled Keith. "I ain't done nothin'."
>
> Jim heard the commotion and turned back. "It's all right, officer," he called reassuringly. "I can explain everything."
>
> The policeman relaxed his grip. Too much. Keith was off in a flash.
>
> "Phew, that was close," said Jim as they hid behind a hedge.

Put speech marks around the words that are spoken.

Vary your words for 'said'.

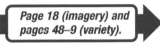

Did You Know?

The initials of J R R Tolkien, the author of *Lord of the Rings*, stand for John Ronald Reuel.

Spot Check

1 What is a 3rd person narrative?
2 'The more characters the better.' True or false?
3 What is the difference between an unfinished story and a cliffhanger ending?
4 Give three rules to follow when including dialogue.

Writing to describe

Descriptive writing

- You may be asked to describe an **event**, **place** or **person**. Your aim is to tell the readers about it in an interesting and entertaining way.

- Descriptions mean giving more than the facts. You have to **bring the event, person or place to life** by using language effectively.

- The description does not have to be true, but it has to be **believable**.

Planning and structure

- If this is the longer writing task, use the planning grid provided.

- A **spider diagram** is good for planning description. Brainstorm **different ideas** on the subject. Then decide on the **order**.

- Start with the main idea in the middle and branch out like this:

size — inside aircraft
seats
meals
take-off
JOURNEY ON AIRCRAFT
main facts — when
where
landing

Descriptive language

- Use the **senses**. Describe what you see, so that others can see it. But also what you smell, hear, touch, taste and feel, e.g.
  I jumped as the elephant lifted its trunk and bellowed.

- Use **powerful words**, especially nouns, verbs and adjectives. Replace dull words with interesting ones, e.g.
  The town ~~was full of~~ rang with the cries of street sellers.

- Include some special **imagery** if you can (similes, metaphors, etc), e.g. *His eyebrows scuttled like spiders across his brow.*

- Go into **detail**. Precise description is more powerful than general comments, e.g.
  I put on my ~~hat~~ thick green bobble hat and opened the door.

- **Vary** the length and type of your sentences.

> **Top Tip!**
> You can use these descriptive techniques in other kinds of writing too, especially writing stories.

Pages 48–9.

Example

This is the beginning of a level 7 description of 'a memorable journey'.

level
7

My first trip on an aeroplane, when I was about six, sticks in my mind. Not because it was dramatic in any obvious way – we were going on holiday to Spain, just like millions of other people – but because it was such a new experience for me.

Everything was strange. Even before we boarded I was transfixed by the vast halls full of people, the suitcases disappearing behind the flaps, as if they were being eaten by a mechanical monster, the brisk uniformed officials who always knew where they were going.

The aircraft itself was rather disappointing: I felt like I had moved from a mansion to a broom cupboard. But as soon as the engines whined and the plane lumbered into position, I was gripped again. Take-off was a punch in the chest, which left me breathless. Out of the window I could see London becoming toytown below me.

- Structure is careful and clear. 1st paragraph gives the background.
- Note the long, well-worked sentence.

- Emphasis on writer's feeling – overwhelmed.
- Powerful words: 'transfixed', 'vast'.
- Simile of monster.
- Good contrast between short and long sentence.

- Effective images: 'mansion', 'punch in the chest', 'toytown'.
- Powerful verbs: 'whined', 'lumbered'.
- Emphasis on seeing and feeling.

Did You Know?

A cliché is a phrase that has been over-used, which makes it dull and lifeless. Examples are 'take the bull by the horns' and 'a blessing in disguise'.

Spot Check

1 Give two reasons why a spider diagram is useful for planning descriptions.
2 Does all the description have to be true?
3 Why are adjectives useful in descriptive writing?
4 What is imagery?

Writing to inform and explain

Structure and planning

- Spider diagrams are useful planning tools when writing **information**. They allow you to brainstorm ideas and group them by topic.

Page 64.

- **Explanation** texts follow a logical structure. A step-by-step planning tool works well, e.g.

- Use **paragraphs** to organise your writing – one paragraph for each bubble on the diagram.

- Use **connectives** to guide the reader through the text and link the paragraphs, e.g. *first, then, in addition, for example, because, as a result, when, therefore.*

- Begin with a clear **introduction**. You can end with a summary.

- Longer information texts may need **subheadings** or **bullet points**.

Content and language

- Information and explanation texts are are fact-based. They need to be clear and concise. Avoid persuasive or highly descriptive language.

- Use **formal** English, in the **3rd person** (unless the facts are about you):
  I hang out in a youth club, but there's another one too. ✗
  Teenagers have the choice of two youth clubs. ✔

Pages 42 and 46.

Top Tip!
Remember your **audience** when writing. Children will need a different approach to (say) parents or older people.

- Begin each paragraph with a **general statement** (topic sentence), then continue with further **detail** or **examples**, e.g.
  Animals can do some extraordinary things. Pumas, for example, can jump up to 20 metres.

- If you are writing a **newspaper report**, include the main facts in the first one or two paragraphs, then fill out background detail later; include quotes and a snappy headline.

Pages 50–1.

This is an extract from a level 7 information sheet, written by a student about their own house, for a 'time capsule'.

level
7

Built in the 1890s from Cotswold stone, the house is attached to both its neighbours, forming a terrace of three. However, there is plenty of space for a family of five, as it is spread over four floors.

The ground floor consists of a small entrance hall which leads to a double-sized living room with an open fire, piano and hi-fi. At one end is a large, kitchen extension; at the other is a south-facing conservatory with a sofa and TV. There is also a downstairs toilet.

On the first floor is a large single bedroom and a bathroom with a walk-in shower. There are two bedrooms on the second floor, one of which is double. At the very top of the house is a converted attic bedroom with a large window in the roof. Three of the bedrooms have fantastic views across the valley; on a clear day you can even see the Black Mountains in Wales.

Language:
– clear and factual – lots of nouns
– consistently written in 3rd person – no 'me' or 'our'
– good range of sentence types to keep interest
– formal English throughout

Structure:
– well-organised, with one topic per paragraph
– topic sentences make it clear what the topic is
– connectives guide the reader, e.g. 'however', 'also'

Did You Know?

English borrows from many other languages, e.g. *hamburger* (German), *kayak* (Eskimo) and *shampoo* (Hindi).

Spot Check

1 'The main aim of an information text is to entertain the reader.' True or false?
2 Why is a step-by-step planning tool useful for explanation texts?
3 What kind of connectives would you expect to include in an explanation text?
4 Give two special features of news reports.

Writing to discuss and review

Structure and planning

- A spider diagram is a useful planning tool for a **review**. Give each feature of the book, film, etc. a different bubble, e.g.
  - for a **book**: plot, characters, language, themes
  - for a **film**: plot, acting, special effects, direction

Page 64.

- Begin with **information** about the product, then **one paragraph per feature**, then **sum up** your view.

- Use the planning tool on the right for a balanced **discussion**.

1 Introduction to issue: ————————————————
2 Points for — 3 Points against
4 Conclusion – summing up (include your view)

- Use **connectives** to guide the reader through the discussion, e.g. *therefore, in addition, on the other hand, however.*

- Make it clear **who holds what views**, e.g. *Other people say …, Opponents argue …*

Language and style

- In **discussion** texts:

  - use **formal** language, e.g. *A view shared by many is that …*

  - give **examples** and **quote** people's views, e.g.
    Sandra, for example, says, 'Smokers should pay for their own hospital bills.' (direct speech)
    Sandra believes that smokers should pay for their own hospital bills. (indirect speech)

  - present people's views **fairly** – put your own view in the **conclusion**.

- In **reviews**:

  - the purpose is to **entertain** as well as **inform**, so your style can be more **lively** and **informal**, e.g.
    Flip to the end and you'll get a shock.

  - cover both the **good and bad points** of the product.

  - include your **own view** throughout, e.g. *I felt that …*

  - write in the **present tense**, e.g. *The special effects are amazing, the characters fail to convince.*

SMOKERS SHOULD PAY FOR THEIR OWN HOSPITAL BILLS.

Pages 47 and 49 (reviews).

Example

This is the start of a discussion which analyses the results of a survey on attitudes to single-sex schools.

Choosing between a single-sex or a mixed school can be quite a dilemma for students as well as parents. And both groups of people are deeply divided on the issue, as the survey shows.

Those who favour single-sex schools, like Louise, often say that they allow students to learn, without getting distracted by romantic attachments. But opponents like Rob argue that most schools in the country are mixed, and plenty of learning goes on in them.

Whether single-sex schools are 'natural' is another issue. Several students think that all-boy or all-girl classes don't reflect real-life situations. However, others, such as Yajnah, point out that schools are unnatural anyway.

 **Top Tip!**

When planning a discussion, instead of grouping all the points 'for' together, followed by all the points 'against', you may like to take each point at a time and explore the views for and against. This approach has been taken in the example here.

Structure:
– clear introduction to the issue
– one paragraph for each point
– good use of connectives to guide reader, eg 'however', 'but opponents …'

Language/style:
– formal language throughout
– balanced approach which doesn't show writer's view
– refers to people's views in detail

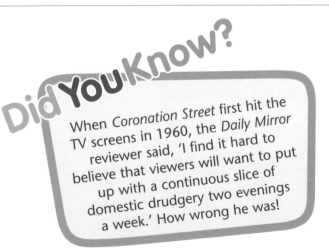

Did You Know?

When *Coronation Street* first hit the TV screens in 1960, the *Daily Mirror* reviewer said, 'I find it hard to believe that viewers will want to put up with a continuous slice of domestic drudgery two evenings a week.' How wrong he was!

Spot Check

1 Which is usually written in more formal language, a discussion or a review?
2 How can you make the structure of a discussion balanced?
3 'You shouldn't include your own opinion in a review.' True or false?
4 Give three connectives that could be useful in a discussion.

Writing to persuade, argue, advise

Structure and planning

- Persuasive writing usually consists of a **series of points** in a **logical order**. This is a useful planning tool:

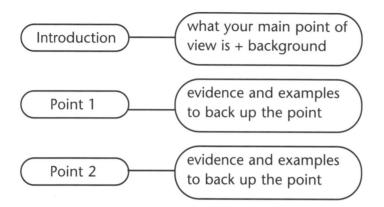

Introduction — what your main point of view is + background

Point 1 — evidence and examples to back up the point

Point 2 — evidence and examples to back up the point

Top Tip!

You can make up quotations from 'experts' to back up your arguments.

- Give each point a **new paragraph**.

- Begin with an **introduction** and end with a powerful **conclusion**.

- **Connectives** are important to join up your ideas, e.g. *therefore, because, firstly*.

Language and style

- If you are writing an argument, you may want to sound **reasonable** (think about the purpose and audience of the task). Use **formal language** and avoid exaggerating.

- Think of your **opponent's arguments** and try to counter them.

- Include some **rhetorical techniques**, e.g.

  - **emotive words**: *starving* (not *hungry*), *children* (not *people*)

  - **repetition**: *it isn't fair and it isn't just*

  - **alliteration**: *a **pr**essing **pr**oblem*

  - **rhetorical questions** (where the answer is obvious): *Are we to take this seriously?*

  - **personal pronouns**: *we* includes the audience, *you* addresses the audience directly

- For **more persuasive** writing, such as a speech encouraging a sports team, include more rhetorical techniques!

Did YOU Know?

Many politicians have professional speech-writers to write their speeches for them.

- When **writing to advise**:

  - Use softer language and a friendly tone, e.g.
    Have you thought about …?

  - Include words like *should, could, may* and *perhaps* to make suggestions.

  - Informal language may be appropriate, depending on the audience, e.g. *Check this out!*

  - Give reasons why your advice should be followed, e.g.
    If you do this, then …

Page 51 (advice texts).

Example

Here is a level 7 piece of writing arguing against banning access to the Internet.

The Internet dangerous? Of course it can be dangerous to let children use some sites and some chat rooms unsupervised. But cars are just as dangerous and we don't ban them, do we?

The point is to make sure that you know what sites your children are using. In programs such as MSM Messenger, for example, users only talk to people who know their email address. You can be sure that your children are chatting to people they can trust, and not some dangerous paedophile.

If you ban access to the Internet, you are preventing your children from using one of the world's great resources. And you are preventing them from learning to behave responsibly.

powerful opening

rhetorical question

new paragraph for each point

example to back up point

emotive words

repetition

Spot Check

1 How do paragraphs help you structure an argument?
2 Give three rhetorical techniques.
3 Which of these adjectives would you avoid in persuasive writing?
   fantastic, wonderful, amazing, good, excellent
4 In what kind of writing are you likely to use words like *would, should* and *may*?

Follow these guidelines to improve your writing from level 6 to level 7.

Structure and organisation

- **Structure** your writing for maximum impact. Make your **introduction** and **conclusion** really count – use a dramatic beginning or surprising ending in a story, for example.

- Make the structure of any argument or discussion crystal clear by using **paragraphs** and **connectives**.

- **Develop** and link the points within each paragraph.

Content

- In **stories**, make sure your characters and dialogue are **believable**.

- In non-fiction, **brainstorm** interesting, thoughtful ideas before you start writing.

Audience and purpose

- Take **audience** and **purpose** into account at all times, e.g.

  – keep up the same level of **formality** that the task demands

  – choose a distinctive **voice** and stick to it throughout.

Language

- Make every word count.

- Use different **sentence structures** for emphasis and variety.

- Use language for **special effects**, e.g. to create tension in a story.

- Make full use of **rhetorical techniques** in persuasive writing.

Top Tip!

Give yourself enough checking time – this is where you can pick up those extra marks.

Punctuation, grammar and spelling

- Use the **full range of punctuation** accurately to structure your sentences and make the meaning clear.

- Make sure there are **no grammatical errors**.

- **Spell** all your words **correctly**, including complex words.

Remember to practise spelling!

Read this level 6 piece of writing, intended to advise students on good study skills. The notes show how it could be raised to a level 7.

level 6

How NOT to study

Do you want to make the <u>worst</u> use of your time when you get down to work? Then simply follow this advice...

- <u>Don't get into a study routine.</u> If you find you are developing a routine, such as studying as soon as you get home from school, then <u>don't.</u> Routines only make it easier to start work. So make sure you don't develop any helpful working habits like this.

- <u>Work non-stop.</u> Regular breaks actually increase your work out put because you return to work refreshed. So keep your nose to your desk for at least three hours at a time, and you will see the benefits, boredom and tiredness.

- <u>Don't get distracted.</u> A noisy place is a disaster if you want to study effectiveley. So avoid doing your studying on the bus, or in the television room with your mobile switched on. The interuptions will seriously distract you from doing any proper work.

A clever idea to turn the advice round like this, but the final paragraph needs to keep the irony up.

Use of words is usually effective, but 'don't' here is dull and repetitive – replace it with 'cut it out'.

Some incorrect spelling loses the student marks: 'output', 'effectively', 'interruption'.

More variety in punctuation needed, e.g. use a dash here instead of a comma.

Paragraphs and bullets used to good effect, but piece needs a good conclusion.

Did You Know?

You can visit Collins Word Exchange to look up any English word in the dictionary, build your own dictionary, join forums to discuss word uses, and test your English skills by playing games: www.collins.co.uk/wordexchange/

The Shakespeare paper

The key things you need to know

- The Shakespeare test lasts 45 minutes. It is worth 18 marks.

- You are given a **question paper**, which contains **one** question. The question focuses on extracts from the set scenes that you have been studying in class. These extracts are provided on the question paper.

- You are also given an **answer booklet**, which is simply lined paper for you to write your answer on.

Top Tip!

You are assessed on how well you understand the scenes, not on the quality of your writing, so mistakes in grammar and spelling do not count against you. However, you need to communicate your understanding, so the better you can express yourself the more marks you are likely to get.

You have to ...

- Answer the precise question given, which will ask you to write about the **scenes** you have been studying. You will not be asked to compare the scenes.

- Base your answer on the **extracts** given, though knowledge of the rest of the play and of Shakespeare's world will be useful.

Pages 76–7.

- Show that you really understand the extracts, by making **points** about them and backing up your points with **quotations**.

Pages 82–3.

What you are assessed on

You will be asked a question about **one** of these four aspects of the play:

- **Character and motivation** – this means you have to understand the behaviour of the main characters. You need to know why the characters behave as they do (motivation).

Pages 84–5.

- **Ideas, themes and issues** – this means you have to understand the particular ideas (such as love or revenge) that the play explores.

Pages 86–7.

- **Language** – this means looking at what Shakespeare's characters say, how they say it and the effect that this has on the audience.

Pages 78–9 and 88–9.

- **Performance** – this means understanding and explaining how the scenes would have been performed, and how you might put them on if you were the director.

Pages 90–1.

- You should spend the first **10 minutes planning** your answer.

Pages 80–1.

- You should spend the last **5 minutes checking** what you have written. This will always gain you marks.

- Your teacher will remind you of the time, e.g. halfway through the test and 5 minutes before the end.

Example

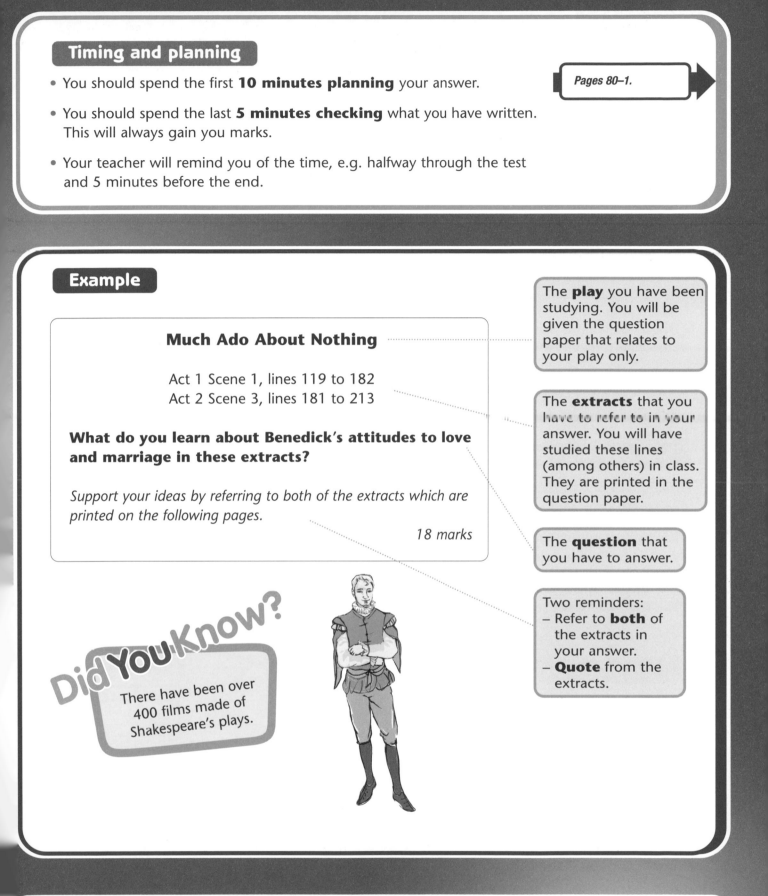

Much Ado About Nothing

Act 1 Scene 1, lines 119 to 182
Act 2 Scene 3, lines 181 to 213

What do you learn about Benedick's attitudes to love and marriage in these extracts?

Support your ideas by referring to both of the extracts which are printed on the following pages.

18 marks

The **play** you have been studying. You will be given the question paper that relates to your play only.

The **extracts** that you have to refer to in your answer. You will have studied these lines (among others) in class. They are printed in the question paper.

The **question** that you have to answer.

Two reminders:
– Refer to **both** of the extracts in your answer.
– **Quote** from the extracts.

Did You Know?

There have been over 400 films made of Shakespeare's plays.

Spot Check

True or false?

1 There is only one Shakespeare paper.
2 You are tested on your historical knowledge about Shakespeare's life and times.
3 You have to refer to all the set scenes in your answer.
4 You should spend 10 minutes planning your answer.

Shakespeare's plays

Tragedy, comedy, history, romance

Shakespeare wrote different kinds of plays:

- **Tragedies** are serious and end with the main character's death. They explore power, jealousy, ambition and love. Examples: *Macbeth, Romeo and Juliet.*

- **Comedies** are light-hearted and have a happy ending. They explore the relationships of men and women in love, and include misunderstandings and disguise. Examples: *Much Ado About Nothing, As You Like It.*

- **Histories** tell the story of English kings. They explore conflict, loyalty and what it means to be a king. Examples: *Richard III, Henry V.*

- **Romances** begin tragically and end happily. They are sometimes called 'tragicomedies'. Examples: *The Tempest, Pericles.*

Shakespeare's world

William Shakespeare (born 1564, died 1616) lived during the reigns of Elizabeth I and James I. The world was very different then:

- **Kings and queens** were all-powerful. People believed they were chosen by God to rule the country.

- The **upper classes** (nobles, e.g. dukes) also had a lot of power. The **lower classes** (ordinary people) had to respect their superiors.

- There was a lot of **political conflict**, including plots against the rulers.

- **Men** had far more power than women.

- People were very **religious** and **superstitious**. They believed in witches and magic.

Top Tip!

If you can refer to your knowledge of Shakespeare or his times in your answer that will gain you marks, but **only if it is relevant** to the question and the set scenes.

The theatre

- The theatre was very **popular** in Shakespeare's day – people had no TV or cinema. All classes of society watched his plays.

- **Stage** and **scenery** were very simple. There were many rough and ready outdoor productions.

- **Masques** (masked balls) were very popular in the reign of James I. They included music, dance, song and 'special effects'. *The Tempest* has masque-like features.

- Plays are divided into **acts** (large sections) and **scenes** (subsections marking a new time or place). They include dialogue and stage directions.

Example

This extract from *The Tempest*, Act 5 Scene 1, shows some of the issues that were important in Shakespeare's day.

PROSPERO But you, my brace of lords, were I so minded,
I here could pluck his highness' frown upon you,
And justify you traitors: at this time
I will tell no tales.
SEBASTIAN [*Aside*] The devil speaks in him.
PROSPERO   No.
For you, most wicked sir, whom to call brother
Would even infect my mouth, I do forgive
Thy rankest fault; all of them; and require
My dukedom of thee, which, perforce, I know,
Thou must restore.

Lords and ladies were key figures in Shakespeare's day, and in his plays.

Treachery – plotting against the crown – was a real issue in the politics of the day.

Everyone believed in **God** and the **Devil**, and thought that there were good and evil spirits.

The plays often end by restoring power to the **rightful ruler**. What made a true ruler was a question much debated.

Did You Know?

Women were not allowed to act in Shakespeare's day, so boys played all the female roles.

Spot Check

1 Why did Shakespeare write about kings?
2 Give two differences between the theatre in Shakespeare's time and today.
3 Give two features of Shakespeare's comedies.

Shakespeare's language

Different kinds of language

- Most of the lines are in **blank verse** (unrhymed poetry). Each line has a regular pattern of **10 syllables**, with emphasis on every other syllable:
  Go, <u>charge</u> my <u>goblins</u> <u>that</u> they <u>grind</u> their <u>joints</u>

- Some passages are in **prose** (ordinary writing), especially when comic characters and the lower classes are speaking: *What have we here? a man or a fish? dead or alive? A fish: he smells like a fish …*

- **Long speeches** are often full of expression and feeling. **Soliloquies** (speeches when the actor is alone on stage) show the audience what the character is thinking and feeling.

- Characters often speak **alternate lines** when they are arguing, e.g.

RICHARD	Then plainly to her tell my loving tale.
ELIZABETH	Plain and not too honest is too harsh a style.
RICHARD	Your reasons are too shallow and too quick.
ELIZABETH	Oh no, my reasons are too deep and dead.

Top Tip!

Reading the script aloud, slowly, will help you to understand it. Do not pause at the end of the lines unless there is a comma or full stop.

Expressive language

- Shakespeare uses **striking vocabulary** (choice of words):
  - to convey a character's **feelings**, e.g. *underhand corrupted foul injustice* (Buckingham about Richard's government, in *Richard III*).
  - to draw a vivid **picture**, e.g. *plunged in the foaming brine* (Ariel about the shipwreck, in *The Tempest*).

- He also uses **word play**, especially in comic scenes:
  Though thou canst swim like a duck, thou art made like a goose (Stephano about Trinculo, in *The Tempest*).

- **Sound effects** such as **alliteration** (repeated sounds) add power to the poetry, e.g. *All sanctimonious ceremonies may*
  With full and holy rite be minister'd (*The Tempest*).

- Shakespeare uses **imagery** to draw word pictures in the minds of the audience:
  - **similes**: *as chaste as is the bud ere it be blown* (*Much Ado About Nothing*)
  - **metaphors**: *that bottled spider who's deadly web ensnareth thee about* (Margaret about Richard, in *Richard III*)
  - **personification**: *The winds did sing it to me, and the thunder* (*The Tempest*)

Unfamiliar features

Shakespeare's language is 400 years old and highly poetic. Look out for these features:

- **old-fashioned words**, e.g. *thee/thou* (= you), *thy* (= your), *hath/hast* (= has)

- **strange word order**, e.g. *Thee of thy son, Alonso, they have bereft* (= They have taken your son away from you, Alonso.)

- **missing letters**, e.g. *'scape* = escape, *shak'd* = shaked (shook). Note that *shak'd* is pronounced as one syllable, *shaked* as two syllables.

Example

The spirit Ariel describes how he casts a spell on the drunken Caliban and his friends (*The Tempest*, Act 4 Scene 1). Note:
- the **similes** – he compares them first to young horses (colts), then to calves following the sound of the mooing of the herd
- the **vivid description** of the scene.

Did You Know?

Many common expressions first appeared in Shakespeare's works, including 'love letter', 'puppy dog', 'wild goose chase' and 'what the dickens'.

> Then I beat my tabor*,
> At which, like unback'd* colts, they prick'd their ears,
> Advanc'd their eyelids, lifted up their noses
> As they smelt music: so I charm'd their ears
> That, calf-like, they my lowing* follow'd through
> Tooth'd briers, sharp furzes, pricking goss and thorns,
> Which enter'd their frail shins: at last I left them
> I' the filthy-mantled* pool beyond your cell,
> There dancing up to the chins, that the foul lake
> O'erstunk their feet.

*drum

*not yet ridden

*mooing

*refers to the stagnant 'coat' on the pool

Spot Check

1 What does 'blank verse' mean?
2 When does Shakespeare use prose?
3 What is alliteration?
4 What two types of imagery are used in this quote from *The Tempest*?
   their great guilt, like poison given to work a great time after, now 'gins to bite the spirits

Understand the question

To give a precise and relevant answer you need to think carefully about what the question is asking you to do. Look at these questions, for example:

How does Caliban's language show his feelings for Prospero?

This question is about Shakespeare's **language**. The focus is on **Caliban's feelings** for Prospero, in *The Tempest*.

What problems would the director have to solve in putting on these scenes?

The question is about **performing** the play. The focus is on **problems** in performance.

What different impressions of Richard do we get in these extracts?

The question is about the **character** of Richard III. The focus is on the **different sides** of his character, including **why** he behaves as he does (his motivation).

Top Tip!
Your essay needs to be **balanced**, so make sure you cover **all the scenes** in your planning.

Re-read the extracts

- Unless you know the set scenes off by heart, you should read the extracts again, with the question in mind.

- **Highlight the key words** or passages that relate to the question.

- Add any short **notes** in the margin that occur to you as you read.

Brainstorm ideas

- Jot down some **key words** or **ideas**, and add some **thoughts** and **quotations** next to them. Use a spider diagram or other planning tool to help you, as in the plan for this question about *Much Ado About Nothing*:

What do you learn about Benedick's attitudes to love and marriage in these extracts?

'professed tyrant' — hates women and marriage — B's attitudes to love and marriage — rude about Claudio and Hero — 'too low for high praise' — doesn't notice Beatrice's rudeness — changes attitude in 2nd extract

- Use this as the **plan** for your answer.

- Decide on the **order** in which you will discuss each main point. **Number** them on your plan.

Example

Here is a completed plan to answer the question:

What impressions do we get of Richard in Act 1 Scene 1 and Act 4 Scene 2?

<u>Intro</u>	– both scenes are key for R's character
<u>Act 1 Scene 1</u>	
sly	– 'imprisonment shall not be long' (to Clarence)
wicked	– 'determined to prove a villain'
angry about being deformed	– 'cheated of feature'
cunning	– 'plots have I laid'
<u>Act 4 Scene 2</u>	
ruthless	– wants to kill princes
	– 'tear-falling pity dwells not'
angry	– Buckingham won't obey him
wicked	– 'I am so far in blood'
cunning	– wants to spread rumours about his wife
<u>Conclusion</u>	– just as bad and cunning later in play, but losing control, getting desperate

Did YOU Know?

The 'Reduced Shakespeare' theatre company have summarised all 37 of Shakespeare's plays and turned them into one fast-moving comedy lasting an hour and a half.

- Note that this plan takes **each scene** in turn.

- If you are confident, you could take **each impression** of Richard in turn, and discuss how he appears cunning, wicked, etc. in both scenes:

> Intro – both scenes are key for R's character
> Cunning – 'plots I have laid' (Act 1) – rumours about wife (Act 4)
> Wicked – 'determined to prove a villain' (Act 1) – 'I am so far in blood' (Act 4), etc.

- This approach is more difficult to follow, but is more focused and impressive when you carry it off.

**Spot Check**

What are these questions asking you to focus on? Match each question with a focus.

Questions	Focus of the question
1 How is the idea of forgiveness explored in the final scene of *The Tempest*?	**a** language
2 Explain whether you think Caliban is foolish in these scenes.	**b** theme
3 How do Ferdinand and Miranda show in their words that they are deeply in love?	**c** performance
4 What advice would you give the actor playing Ariel in these scenes?	**d** character

Begin and end effectively

- Begin with an **introduction**. This should:
  - show that you **understand the question**, without giving a detailed answer.
  - refer to the **key words** in the question, e.g. *Hero's language* or *Caliban's feelings.*
  - refer to the **context**, e.g. *in these scenes* or *in Act 1 Scene 3*

- The final paragraph should be a **conclusion**. This should:
  - return to the **focus** of the question, e.g. *Hero's language, therefore, …*
  - draw together the **key points**, e.g. *We have seen that Caliban's feelings are wide-ranging: first he is …*

Refer to the extracts

- Often you can **summarise** or **paraphrase** the evidence. This means using your own words, e.g. *Antonio suggests a brutal plot to murder the sleeping king.*

- You also need to **quote directly** from the extracts. This helps you make your point, and shows the examiners that you understand the play. Use **inverted commas** to show you are quoting.

- You can embed **short quotations** in your sentences, e.g. *In a powerful image, Ariel describes Ferdinand's hair as standing up 'like reeds'.*

- **Longer quotations** should start a new line, and be indented. Keep them as short as you can but still make your point.

- Remember: **Point – Evidence – Comment**. Begin by making your own point, in your own words. Then quote from the extract to back up your point. Finally, use your own words to explain how the quotation backs up your point.

> **Top Tip!**
> For each main point that you make in your answer, give a quotation from the extracts and explain why it is relevant.

Page 83.

Write well

- **Write clearly**. Use one paragraph per point. Use connectives to link your ideas, e.g. *in addition, by contrast, also, however.*

- **Write with style.** Make your answer stand out from the others. Think of interesting words to use, vary your sentence structure and be bold in expressing your opinion.

- Keep your tone **formal**.

- Don't just give a brief discussion of each point – **develop your points** in a thoughtful and convincing way so that your answer thoroughly **analyses** the issue.

Did You Know?
You can rearrange the letters in 'William Shakespeare' to make 'I am a weakish speller'.

Example

This is the beginning of an answer to the question:

How does Shakespeare make the audience laugh in Act 2 Scene 2 and Act 3 Scene 2 of *The Tempest*?

Shakespeare uses all sorts of skills in these scenes to make the audience laugh. His characters are amusing, the language they use is funny, and there is a lot of slapstick and misunderstanding.

At the beginning of the first extract Caliban thinks that Trinculo is a spirit sent by Prospero to torment him. This is deliberately funny, as Trinculo is only a jester. Shakespeare could have cleared the misunderstanding up very quickly by making Caliban realise that Trinculo is not a spirit, but he keeps the idea going for a long time. When Stephano sings his song, Caliban yells 'Do not torment me: O!' and he repeats this after Stephano's next speech. Each time Caliban makes this mistake, the audience will roar with laughter.

Introduction:
– Refers to the key words in the question ('make the audience laugh').
– Refers to the context ('these scenes').
– Gives a summary of the key points, which will be developed in the answer.

Reference to the extract without using a quotation, but still with a comment.

Point – misunderstanding is kept going.
Evidence – 'Do not torment me: O!'
Comment – why it is effective.

Answer is **well organised** (one paragraph for the first main point), **clear** and **well written**.

Stephano forces Caliban to drink while Trinculo hides under the covers (from Act 2 Scene 2, *The Tempest*). This photograph is from a modern interpretation performed by the Royal Shakespeare Company.

Spot Check

1 Give two things that an introduction should do.
2 Why should you quote directly from the extracts?
3 What does 'Point – Evidence – Comment' help you to remember?
4 What are these connectives useful for?
  in the same way, similarly, too, also

Answering questions on characters

Revising for questions on characters

You may be asked to describe how a character behaves in the set scenes, or what is going on in a relationship. In order to prepare for a question like this:

- **Draw up a character log** for the characters in your play, with brief descriptions of who they are. Some of this could be in the form of a family tree, e.g.

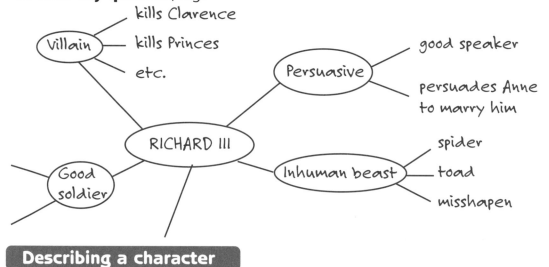

Queen Margaret
(mother-in-law of
Lady Anne)

Duchess of York
mother of:

Queen Elizabeth (marries) Edward IV   Clarence (murdered by R.)   Richard III (Duke of Gloucester)   (marries) Lady Anne (murdered by R.)

Young Princes (murdered by R.)

- Take two or three of the main characters and compile a **spider diagram of their key qualities**, e.g.

RICHARD III

Villain — kills Clarence / kills Princes / etc.

Persuasive — good speaker / persuades Anne to marry him

Inhuman beast — spider / toad / misshapen

Good soldier

Describing a character

When describing what a character is like, refer to:

- **what they say,** e.g. *Caliban acts like a slave. He says, 'I will kiss thy foot.'*

- **what they do**, e.g. *Caliban shows Prospero 'all the qualities o' th' isle'.*

- **what others say** about them, e.g. *Trinculo calls him 'a most ridiculous monster'.*

- **why they behave** as they do (their motivation), e.g. *Caliban wanted to kill Prospero so that he could live on his island as a free man.*

Top Tip!

Whenever you make a point about a character, back it up with a quote from the extracts.

Remember that characters can **change** in the course of the play, e.g. Richard loses control of events the more that he plots and kills, in *Richard III*.

Writing in role

Occasionally you are asked to write as if you were one of the characters of the play. This means you have to:

- get under the skin of your character, by **imagining what it feels** like to be them in that situation.

- **stay in role** – refer to yourself throughout as 'I' and 'me' and keep that pretence going.

- **explain** what you are doing, thinking and feeling and why (your motivation).

- **quote** from the set scenes to back up what you say.

Did You Know?

The largest speaking part in all of Shakespeare's plays is Hamlet (nearly 1500 lines).

Example

This is the start of a level 7 answer to the question:

What impressions do we get of Benedick in Act 1 Scene 1 and Act 2 Scene 3 of *Much Ado About Nothing*?

level 7

> Although he maintains certain elements of his character, Benedick gives quite different impressions to the audience in the two scenes.
>
> In the first scene we see Benedick with other people. He is showing off, and so comes across as arrogant and vain. For example, he 'thanks' his mother for giving birth to him and bringing him up, but asks that 'all women' excuse him from being tied down as a husband. This is because he doesn't want to be ruled or controlled by them. He says, 'Shall I never see a bachelor of three score again?', and he calls marriage a 'yoke', which is a harness to control horses.
>
> Benedick also comes across as a joker in Act 1 Scene 1. He is keen to display his wit and entertain others. For example ...

Good introduction: summarises the answer and uses the key word 'impressions'.

Commenting on what Benedick does.

Commenting on what Benedick says.

Commenting on why he behaves as he does.

Quotations are well chosen and carefully included in the answer.

A new paragraph for the new point.

Spot Check

Choose two of the main characters in your play. Draw up a spider diagram for each one, to display their key features or qualities.

Answering questions on ideas and themes

Knowing the story

- You won't be asked to discuss the **plot** (the story of the whole play), but you do need to know about the **key events** to understand the play and how the set scenes fit in to the whole.

- Draw up a **storyline** to remind yourself of the plot, like this one about *The Tempest*:

    Act 1   The shipwreck

                 Prospero tells Miranda about his past

                 The history of the spirit Ariel is described

                 Prospero and Miranda visit Caliban

Did You Know?

William Shakespeare was the first person to refer to a coward as 'chicken'.

Top Tip!

If you are asked about a theme, relate it to the scenes provided. Remember to back up your ideas with quotes from the extracts.

Themes

Themes are the **main ideas** explored in a play:

The Tempest

- **forgiveness** – Prospero and his enemies, Caliban and Prospero
- **civilisation** – the 'savage' Caliban compared with the 'civilised' dukes
- **master and servant** – Caliban/Ariel and Prospero, Gonzalo and Alonso
- **magic** – Prospero a 'good' magician, Ariel a spirit

Much Ado About Nothing

- **love and marriage** – Benedick and Beatrice, Hero and Claudio
- **tricks and deception** – e.g. Benedick is tricked to make him fall in love
- **honour and status** – e.g. Hero's 'unfaithfulness' shames her father, Leonato
- **role of women** – Beatrice is powerless as a woman, daughters ruled by fathers

Richard III

- **hatred and evil** – Richard is full of both, but fascinating to the audience
- **blame and guilt** – blames others for misfortunes and guilty conscience for killings
- **deception** – Richard deceives Buckingham, Clarence, Anne, Hastings
- **role of women** – their lack of power, the human cost of war

You could be asked to discuss how a single theme is explored in the extracts.

Preparing for a question on theme

- Draw up a spider diagram for each theme of your play. Add detail as you study it, e.g.

Prospero a 'good' witch – uses powers to serve good

brings Ferdinand and Miranda together

arranges for a reconciliation with Antonio

Magic in 'The Tempest'

Caliban's mother Sycorax a 'bad' witch

Ariel a spirit with magic powers

Context – people believed in magic –James I wrote about witchcraft

Example

This is the start of a level 7 answer to the question:

What different ideas about women are explored in Act 1 Scene 1 and Act 2 Scene 3 of *Much Ado About Nothing*?

level 7

Shakespeare's ideas about women in these two scenes reflect the different ways in which they were regarded in his own day.

In the first scene, women are talked about in two very different ways. First of all married women are laughed at and criticised a lot. Benedick complains that marriage is like a 'yoke' (a horse's harness) that gives the married man no freedom. He is left to 'sigh away Sundays', which is a good description of wasting time at home. Women are also attacked for betraying their husbands – Benedick complains of not wanting horns on his forehead, which was a sign of being two-timed.

Alongside this criticism, however, there is a lot of praise heaped on young, beautiful women who come from good families. Claudio calls Hero 'the sweetest lady that ever I looked on'. Clearly young women could also be objects of attraction!

Good **introduction**: summarises the answer and uses the key words 'ideas about women'.

'In the first scene' and 'first of all' help to **organise** and '**signpost**' the answer.

Quotations are well chosen and carefully included in the answer.

New paragraph for a new point.

Note **Point – Evidence – Comment**.

Throughout the focus is on **ideas about women** in the **two** scenes given.

Spot Check

Choose two of the main themes of your play. Draw up a spider diagram for each one, showing how the theme is explored in different scenes and by different characters.

Answering questions on language

Questions on language

- You may be asked to focus on the language used in the set scenes. For example:

  How does Caliban's language show that he is fearful …?

  How do the characters use language to battle with each other …?

  How does Shakespeare build up a mood of tension …?

- You need to explain what the language shows, and **what effect** it has.

Top Tip!

Annotate a copy of your set scenes to show:
- what the language is actually saying
- the effect of language features.

What the language shows

- Think about what the language is actually saying. Each sentence will have a **purpose**, which could include:
  - to persuade
  - to flatter
  - to deceive
  - to hurt
  - to fill in the background for the audience.

- When commenting on a sentence, **explain** what its purpose is, e.g.
  - *Buckingham reflects bitterly on how he has been treated when he says, 'Repays he my deep service with such contempt?'*
  - *Ariel asks, 'Was't well done?' because he is trying to gain Prospero's favour so that he can be freed.*

What effect the language has

- You also need to comment on **how well** the language performs its purpose. Focus on Shakespeare's **expressive language**:

Pages 78–9.

  - **imagery**, e.g. *Margaret's description of Richard as a 'bottled spider' is very accurate, as he lures his victims into his web of deceit.*

  - **powerful words**, e.g. *Buckingham emphasises how bad Richard's government is by piling up the adjectives: 'underhand corrupted foul injustice'.*

  - **sound effects**, e.g. *Caliban almost spits his curse on Prospero (note the repeated 's' sounds): 'all the infections that the sun sucks up'.*

  - **word play**, e.g. *The two halves of Clarence's line show how he is getting two different impressions of the murderer: 'Thy voice is thunder, but thy looks are humble'.*

This is the start of a level 7 answer to the question:

Comment on the purpose and effect of these lines from Act 1 Scene 1 of *Richard III*.

Now are our brows bound with victorious wreaths;
Our bruised arms hung up for monuments;
Our stern alarums changed to merry meetings,
Our dreadful marches to delightful measures.
Grim-visag'd war hath smooth'd his wrinkled front;
And now, instead of mounting barbed steeds,
To fright the souls of fearful adversaries,
He capers nimbly in a lady's chamber,
To the lascivious pleasing of a lute.

Did You Know?

Some of Shakespeare's plays are written completely in verse, such as *King John*, *Richard II* and *Henry VI Part 1*.

level 7

In this opening scene of the play Richard is telling the audience that the war in England has ended. However, this is not merely a factual description, as Richard describes the outbreak of peace using rhetorical devices such as contrast and personification.

the **purpose** of the language

In the first four lines of the extract Richard draws a very effective contrast between war and peace. The contrast is helped by the way he uses images of war in the first half of the lines and images of peace in the second half, for example 'stern alarums' (battle cries) have been changed to 'merry meetings'. Both images relate to a noisy gathering. In the next line the 'dreadful marches' and 'delightful measures' (dances) both relate to movement. The effect is heightened by the alliteration of 'm' throughout.

the **effect** of the language – commenting on the contrast

effective use of **quotation** throughout

In the next few lines Richard develops one particular image – the personification of war as a warrior who replaces fighting with dancing with the ladies. It's a dramatic and effective contrast again, emphasised by the heaviness of the sounds of war ('mounting barbed steeds') followed by the light tripping of the 'l' sounds in the final lines.

the **effect** of the language – commenting on the image

Answering questions on performance

In the director's chair

The question may ask you to **imagine that you are directing** the set scenes, e.g.

What advice would you give to the actor playing Richard?

How would you direct the scene to bring out the conflict between the lovers?

How would you build up tension in these scenes?

- As a director, you need to think about these aspects of the performance:
  - most importantly, the **acting** – how the actors say their lines, move about the stage and relate to other characters
  - the **set** and **costume design**, **lighting** and **sound**.

Answering the question

As you are the director, the ideas are up to you. However:
- You must **explain** why you are directing in a particular way. That means understanding what the characters are doing and why, e.g.
  He should sink to the ground at this point. ✗
  He is in complete despair, so he should sink to the ground at this point. ✓

- You must **link your ideas with the text** by quoting, e.g.
  When Claudio says 'She is the sweetest lady' he should put his and on his heart to show how much love he feels.

> **Top Tip!**
> Remember that Shakespeare wrote his plays to be performed, not to be read. Imagine the actors on stage as they say their lines – how could they best bring out the meaning of their words?

Focus on character, mood and development

- Bring out the **feelings** or **key features** of the character in your direction, e.g. *To show her <u>disgust</u> with Richard, Anne should push him away with her words 'Foul devil'.*

- **Emphasise** a particular **mood** by varying the voice, or pace, or adding pauses, e.g. *Richard should <u>pause</u> with a <u>fixed smile</u> after saying 'and seem a saint', before <u>snarling</u> 'when most I play the devil'.*

- Show that a character or mood can **develop** or **change** through a scene, e.g. *Only when Ferdinand kneels before his father can Alonso believe that it is really him. His voice should show this by …*

Here is part of a level 7 answer to the question:

How would you direct Caliban in *The Tempest* Act 1 Scene 2 to bring out his relationship with Prospero?

Caliban should run onto the stage, hurling his curse at Prospero. Even after Prospero's response, which promises punishment, he should be defiant when he says 'This island's mine'. He should point accusingly at Prospero at 'Which thou takest from me'. This will underline how angry he feels with Prospero at losing his independence.

saying how Caliban should move

saying how Caliban should speak

point – evidence – comment, explaining the direction

Prospero and Caliban threaten and curse each other vehemently (Act 1 Scene 2, *The Tempest*).

Did You Know?

Shakespeare knew how to write for actors because he was an actor as well as a playwright.

Spot Check

True or false?
1 Shakespeare's plays were written to be read on the page.
2 When you are asked to be a director, you have to put on a performance.
3 You don't have to describe how the scenes would have been performed in Shakespeare's day.
4 You can include thoughts on the best lighting and sound.
5 You don't have to quote from the extracts in this kind of question.

To raise your level from level 6 to level 7 in the Shakespeare paper, follow these guidelines.

Show your understanding

- Really think about how the **characters' speech and actions** relate to the main idea that you have to discuss. For example, if the question is about your impressions of Caliban, then think hard about how Caliban comes across in **every detail**.

- Focus on the **effect of Shakespeare's language**. Explain in detail how individual words and phrases show things about the character's feelings or thoughts, or about the wider ideas in the play, e.g.
The phrase 'great master' shows how much Ariel is a slave to Prospero.

- Cover all the **main ideas** that you can think of, across **both extracts**.

- Don't be afraid of including **your own opinion**, as long as you can back it up.

- **Focus on the extracts** given, but try to show through your comments that you understand how they fit into the **play as a whole**, e.g.
As we see later in the play …

Structure your answer

- **Plan** your answer, so that it is well organised and clear.

- Begin with a short **introduction** that sets the scene and refers to the key words in the question.

- End with a **conclusion** that sums up your answer to the question.

- Use **paragraphs** and **connectives** to show how your ideas are organised and linked, e.g. *When we come to Act 3, however, …*

- **Quote** from the extracts frequently, but only **to back up your points**. Short, embedded quotations are better than long quotations. Give a **comment** explaining why the quotation makes your point.

Top Tip!

Only tell the story of the scene (the plot) if it is relevant to the point you are making.

Look at the beginning of this level 7 answer to the question:

What impressions do we get of Richard in Act 1 Scene 1 and Act 3 Scene 7?

level
7

On the surface, it would seem that the impression given by Richard in these two extracts is entirely the same. He tells us in Act 1 Scene 1 that he is 'determined to be a villain', and later, in Act 3 Scene 3, we see him doing precisely that. But is it that simple?

In Act 1 Scene 1 Richard has returned from war, and believes he is not cut out for the 'sportive tricks' of peace. He tells us that he is not handsome, and feels that he has been 'cheated by nature' because of his ugly appearance. He tells us that dogs bark at him and we may even feel a bit sorry for this man who has been dealt such an unfair hand.

Our impression changes, however, as the scene gets going. We learn that because he cannot show love and decency he will follow evil – to 'entertain' himself! He has laid plots, including getting his brother Clarence imprisoned. Our impression is that this man will stop at nothing. As he says himself, he is 'subtle, false and treacherous'.

Good introduction – covers both extracts and refers to key words in question.

Good paragraph organisation – new point for each paragraph.

Tight focus throughout on impressions of Richard.

Notes effect on audience/writer.

Shows an understanding of character development over the scene.

Quotations are brief but relevant, and skilfully included in the sentences.

Did You Know?

William Shakespeare had eleven different ways of spelling his name.

Glossary

adjective a describing word, e.g. 'red', 'evil'

advice a text type which has the aim of suggesting a course of action

alliteration the effect created when words next to each other begin with the same letter (e.g. 'terrible twins')

analyse to investigate something carefully and thoroughly

apostrophe a punctuation mark used to show either possession (e.g. 'Dave's computer') or a missing letter (e.g. 'can't')

argument a text that presents and develops a particular point of view

audience someone who listens to or reads a text

bias weighting a text unfairly in favour of one side or the other

blank verse in Shakespeare's plays, unrhymed verse with 10 syllables in each line

characterisation how an author presents and develops their characters

clause a group of words in a sentence which expresses a single idea; a clause has a verb and usually a subject

colon a punctuation mark that introduces a clause that leads on from or explains another clause

comedy a Shakespearean play about relationships with a happy ending

command a verb that gives an instruction to the reader, e.g. '<u>Think</u> about your children …'

complex sentence a sentence with one main clause and one or more subordinate clauses

compound sentence a sentence made up of two or more simple sentences linked by 'and', 'but' or 'or'

connective a word or phrase which links clauses and sentences, to signal to the audience where the text is going

direct address using the second person ('you') to hold the reader's attention in a text

discussion a text type which helps the audience understand an issue by presenting the different viewpoints fairly

emotive language words, phrases and ideas designed to make the audience feel something strongly

explanation a text type which helps the audience understand why or how something is as it is

fact a piece of knowledge or information that can be proved to be true

fiction anything that is made up, especially a story

formal language writing or speech that follows the strictest rules of Standard English

homophone a word that sounds the same as another but is spelt differently, e.g. 'where' and 'wear'

imagery the use of language to create an image or picture; *see also* simile, metaphor, personification

informal language language that does not follow the strict rules of Standard English

information a text type which presents facts in a way that is easy to understand

instruction a text type which tells the audience how to do something, through a series of sequenced steps

inverted comma a punctuation mark used to show the beginning and end of direct speech

media the term given to texts aimed at large numbers of people, e.g. television, magazines, newspapers, Internet

metaphor a type of imagery which describes something as something else, e.g. 'you are an island'

motivation why a character behaves as he or she does

non-fiction   any text that is not made up

opinion   a person's own view about something

paragraph   a group of sentences on one topic, person or event. A new paragraph begins a new line.

paraphrase   to summarise part of the text in your own words

person   a way of referring to pronouns and verbs according to whether they indicate the speaker/writer (1st person: 'I', 'we'), the audience (2nd person: 'you') or someone else (3rd person: 's/he', 'it', 'they')

personification   a type of imagery which refers to objects as if they were human, e.g. 'the sun punished them'

persuasion   a text type which has the aim of selling an idea or a product

phrase   a group of words which go together, e.g. 'the garden gate'

plot   the storyline

popular newspaper   a newspaper that aims to entertain as much as to inform its readers, e.g. *The Sun, The Mirror*

prefix   letters added at the start of a word to change its meaning

punctuation   a way of marking text with symbols to make the meaning clear

purpose   the aim of a text

recount   a text type which tells the reader what happened, often in an informative and entertaining way

relative clause   part of the sentence beginning 'who', 'which', 'that' etc. which gives more information about the main clause

rhetorical question   a question asked for effect, not for an answer

rhetorical technique   a technique used to persuade an audience, e.g. emotive language, sound effects, repetition,

rhetorical questions

romance   a Shakespearean play that mixes elements of tragedy and comedy

scan   to look over a text quickly in order to find a particular word or piece of information

semi-colon   a punctuation mark used to show a pause in a sentence longer than a comma

simile   a type of imagery which compares something with something else, making the comparison clear by using a phrase such as 'like; or 'as if', e.g. 'she swam like a fish'

simple sentence   a sentences with only one clause

skim   to read a whole text quickly

slogan   a memorable phrase used to sell a product

Standard English   the type of spoken and written English that is generally considered 'correct' and that is taught in schools

suffix   letters added at the end of a word to change its meaning

summarise   to identify the key points of a text

text   a block of spoken or written language

theme   the underlying ideas or issues that a story or play deals with

tone   a measure of the quality, mood or style of a piece of writing

topic sentence   the main sentence in a paragraph, which gives the topic (subject) of the paragraph

tragedy   a Shakespearean play with an unhappy ending

verb   a word that refers to an action, e.g. 'runs' or a state of being, e.g. 'feels'

Index